W9-CES-862

Great Americana

Two Years in the
New Settlements of Ohio

D. Griffiths, Jr.

Two Years
in the New Settlements
of Ohio

by D. Griffiths, Jr.

READEX MICROPRINT

COPYRIGHT © READEX MICROPRINT CORPORATION, 1966

ALL RIGHTS RESERVED

LIBRARY OF CONGRESS CATALOG CARD NO. 66-26343

MANUFACTURED IN THE UNITED STATES OF AMERICA

917.713
G855t

Foreword

The large number of emigrants pouring into the Ohio River Valley in the early 19th century prompted many enterprising writers to publish books offering advice and counsel to others who might contemplate settlement in the West. Such a book was *Two Years' Residence in the New Settlement of Ohio*, written by D. Griffiths, Jr. and published in London, 1835.

Griffiths, an Englishman, wrote primarily for the benefit of his fellow countrymen. Many people, he said, who had "struggled for a living long enough in their native land" were asking, "Where shall we go to better our circumstances?" Griffiths suggested settlement in the Western Reserve of Ohio. To help them, he proposed to supply "all the information which an intelligent emigrant will require respecting the voyage, and journey up the country...how he must proceed to obtain employment, when he arrives in Ohio; the occupations in which as a farmer, he will be engaged; and the manners, customs, religion &c. of the people among whom he intends to cast in his lot."

Griffiths relates that he had himself embarked

31816

at Liverpool in 1832 for New York, voyaging steerage class with some forty others. He describes with touches of humor the cramped, uncomfortable conditions which he and his fellow passengers endured. At New York, he purchased a ticket for a trip up the Hudson River to Albany aboard a steam packet. At Albany, he transferred to canal boat and proceeded through the Erie Canal to Buffalo. There he sailed by steamboat to Cleveland, Ohio.

Having explained in this manner how one might reach the Western Reserve, Griffiths then described for his readers what they might expect to find there. In general his comments were laudatory. Economic opportunities abounded and the life was attractive. The emigrant need not fear that he would be treated with contempt by persons higher in society. "It is a common saying among the farmers of the Western Reserve, 'If a man is good enough to work for me, he is good enough to eat with me.'" Nor should the emigrant hesitate because he had heard of the existence of slavery in the United States. "He shall not hear the 'smack of the whip, and the responding cry of slaves' when he arrives in Ohio," Griffiths explained, because the law prohibited slavery in that region.

Griffiths extolled the high level of education available to the youth of Ohio and detailed, approvingly, the activities of the Temperance Society. He also noted with satisfaction the seriousness with which so many of the inhabitants viewed their religion. Many began their Sabbath exercises on Saturday evening and did not terminate them until sundown on the Sabbath.

A minor irritant for Englishmen, he admitted, was the celebration of Independence Day on July 4. This "annual repetition of injuries, sustained during the Revolutionary War, is too well calculated to keep alive the bitter feeling of Americans towards the British Government ... and on this account is to be lamented."

A chapter by Ralph Leslie Rusk on "Travel and Observation," in *The Literature of the Middle Western Frontier* (New York, 1962), I, 79-130 helps place Griffiths' book in the context of others like it published at approximately the same time.

Two Years in the
New Settlements of Ohio

TWO YEARS' RESIDENCE

IN THE

NEW SETTLEMENTS OF OHIO.

LOG HOUSE.

TWO YEARS' RESIDENCE

IN THE

NEW SETTLEMENTS OF OHIO,

North America:

WITH DIRECTIONS TO EMIGRANTS.

———

By D. GRIFFITHS. Jun.

———

LONDON:

WESTLEY AND DAVIS; JACKSON AND WALFORD;
TOLLER, KETTERING;
ABEL AND WHEELER, NORTHAMPTON;
TOMALIN AND POTTS, DAVENTRY,

———

1835.

KETTERING: PRINTED BY JOSEPH TOLLER.

PREFACE.

WHATEVER political economists may think about emigration as a public relief, it cannot be denied that many English labourers have found it to be a private advantage ; and others are preparing to follow their example.

Where shall we go to better our circumstances ? is the question with numbers who think they have struggled for a living long enough in their native land. In reply to this question, it is not the design of the writer to compare the advantages presented by the different colonies of the world to English emigrants ; nor to lead those who contemplate emigration over all the States of America ; lest, when they lay the book aside, they should find, that by an attempt to teach them every thing, they have learned nothing ; but it is his intention to give

such readers a plain account of the New Settlements on the Western Reserve, which is a section
of Ohio, certainly among the most eligible for
agricultural emigrants; and Ohio itself is always
reckoned one of the best and most inviting States,
embraced by the Great Valley of the Mississippi.

All the information which an intelligent emigrant
will require respecting the voyage, aud journey
up the country, he may find in this publication.
How he must proceed to obtain employment, when
he arrives in Ohio; the occupations in which as a
farmer, he will be engaged; and the manners,
customs, religion &c. of the people among whom
he intends to cast in his lot, are described, with as
much simplicity as possible.

The writer might, indeed, have enlarged upon
the statistics of Ohio, its laws &c. but all this the
emigrant will learn much better in Ohio itself; and
it will be time enough for him to know how he
must proceed with regard to naturalization, when
he has made up his mind to lay his bones in the
New World.

But whilst the work is designed primarily for
emigrants, the writer has not forgotten those of his
readers who think it better still to "dwell in the

land," although many of their friends have emigrated. By familiar description, by dialogues &c. he has endeavoured to bring such readers into the very midst of men and things, as they appear in the New Settlements of America in general, and of Ohio in particular; to give them a just idea of that country, which cannot but be interesting to them as the residence of their children, relatives, and friends.

And to those who have no further object in reading such publications as this than the acquirement of general knowledge, the writer trusts, that the description here presented of country life in America will not be altogether destitute of information.

LONG BUCKBY, *February*, 1835.

CHAPTER I.

" As slow our ship her foaming track
  Against the wind was cleaving,
Her trembling pennant still look'd back
  To that dear isle 'twas leaving.

" So loath we part from all we love,
  From all the links that bind us;
So turn our hearts where'er we rove,
  To those we've left behind us."

In company with about forty other Steerage-passengers, the writer embarked at Liverpool on the 28th of March, 1832, and on the 4th of May following landed at New York. The first week after leaving Liverpool we made but little progress, being detained by contrary winds; but upon the whole it was called a favourable voyage.

The Steerage of the Vessel in which we sailed was about eighteen feet square, and seven feet high; the descent to it, as usual, being by a ladder, and through a hole called the hatchway, which was covered over in rough weather with a kind of lid called the hatch. All the light that found its way below was transmitted through the said hatchway, with the exception of a few rays that struggled through two pieces

B

of thick glass fixed in the roof or deck. Around the sides of the Steerage were two tier of births, one above another like packing-cases; into which, and out of which, the passengers crept night and morning, sometimes stem and sometimes stern foremost. From the roof hung hats and hams; bonnets, onions, and frying-pans; boots and red-herrings; and whatever else might be useful in a sea-voyage; all in perpetual motion. While to the floor of the Steerage were nailed provision-boxes &c., which served the passengers for chairs and tables, as well as cupboards.

Now the reader will easily imagine that forty human beings confined to such a place as this, with the advantages of health and fair weather to boot, must be subject to some inconveniences " shut from the common air and common use of their own limbs." But when head-winds and the dark days come on, alas! for the poor Steerage-passenger.

A certain author, speaking from experience, describes Cabin-passengers as " prisoners, with the chance of being drowned ;" but the situation of passengers in the Steerage, on some occasions, reminded us more of patients in a hospital, with neither doctor nor nurse : and they seemed to care but little whether they were drowned or not. Morning comes, but not a word is uttered, much less a joke; not a passenger stirs. Hear what a hurly there is above ! No hope of lighting a fire such a morning as this. By and bye, a poor fellow, enfeebled with sickness, staggers to the ladder, and if he doesn't get beaten back by a breaker, dashing down the hatchway, he gains the deck. But, on deck every thing is wet, cold, and comfortless. He finds no pity there; the waves drench him, the ship shakes him, and the sailors laugh at him: if he has read Milton, he may feel disposed to soliloquize in the language attributed to the fallen Archangel :—

" Me miserable ! which way shall I fly ?"

During the day, however, some of us kept the deck from preference, consoling one another, as well as we could, with remarks on the sublimity of the scene &c. I must confess that it was rather cold comfort; and we were glad enough when night came to go down below.

On ordinary occasions, there is no lack of impediment to sleep; the rocking of the ship, the sea thundering at our wooden walls for admittance, the creaking of births, and the fear of being pitched out of them, the salt water oozing through upon our beds, the perpetual tinkling of pendent pots and kettles, the tramping of the watch above, and their hallooing at the forecastle every four hours to rouse up the snoring tars to duty on deck, &c., was enough to keep a landsman awake, until habit had rendered such sounds familiar. But, in addition to all this, we had sometimes the bawling of children &c. &c. which might defy Morpheus himself " to steep one's senses in forgetfulness." One night, in particular, during a stiff gale, or, what we land-lubbers called a storm, in spite of nails and cords, the boxes were shaken from the foremast, and tumbled about the floor as if they were be-witched; the storm howled above and around with "deafening clamours;" and amid the up-roar of the elements might be heard, at intervals, the Captain shouting through his speaking-trumpet, or the oaths and curses of the bewil-dered seamen mingling fearfully with the tempest.

With respect to eating, if a man be "more nice than wise," he will not much relish his din-ner, at first, in the Steerage of a Packet-Ship. A few days' voyage, however, rather blunts the edge of one's delicacy; and a week's sea-sick-ness imparts an appetite that despises trifles. The pieces of rice-pudding that were sometimes devoured, when we could get room at the stove on deck, to boil it, would appear truly formidable ashore. But then the reader must bear in mind that Steerage-passengers eat prospectively; for if it happens to turn out a squally day, cooking is out of the question, both for man and woman; and they content themselves as well as they can by crunching hard biscuits. Indeed, the ship's cook himself often found it difficult to provide any thing decent for the Cabin-passengers, not-withstanding the conveniences of the galley; and many a curse did he get from his tyrant, the black steward, for spoiling the dinner.

But gloomy as the steerage-passage is in

squally weather, no sooner did the clouds clear off, and the sun break through into the steerage, than all troubles were forgotten; the floor was cleaned, good humour revived, and the passengers turned out on deck like bees in Spring. Some stand about the stove, cooking, or wait their turn at the fire. Others take a walk round the jolly-boat, which I may call the ship's farm-yard, and talk to the cow, or sheep, or pigs, or poultry in their several tongues; or, they sit upon the water-barrels amusing themselves with a book, or, by the aid of tobacco fumes, wonder what sort of a world it is they are bound for, and build castles in the air. Here they pace the deck, or mount the rigging, or haul in with the seamen, for exercise; and there they gather about a fellow-passenger, who helps them pass away time by a tune on the flute or the fiddle.

Nor are there wanting on board occasional bursts of merriment. A frolic of the wind would jirk a shower of salt water in the face of some fair dame on quarter-deck, proving satisfactorily to the Steerage-passengers at least, if not to the drenched lady herself, that there is no respect of persons with the winds and the waves. Or a sudden lurch of the vessel dashes the batter over a poor fellow frying pancakes, or turns over another's dinner on the steerage floor, after all the trouble of cooking, and in spite of the well known caution, " Hold on!"

It is true, indeed, we had not so many things to take care of as the Cabin-passengers, if the following animated description of a cabin-dinner be correct. " The only thing which forced a smile upon me during the first week of the passage, was the achievement of dinner. In rough weather it is as much as one person can do to keep his place at the table at all; and to guard the dishes, bottles, and castors from a general slide in the direction of the lurch, requires a sleight and coolness reserved only for a sailor. 'Prenez garde,' shouts the Captain as the sea strikes, and in the twinkling of an eye every thing is seized and held up to wait for the other lurch in attitudes which it would puzzle the pencil of Johnson to exaggerate. With his plate of soup in one hand, and the larboard end of the tureen in the other, the claret bottle between his teeth, and the crook of his elbow caught round the mounting corner of the table, the Captain maintains his seat upon the transom, and with a look of the most grave concern, keeps a wary eye on the shifting level of his vermicili; the old weather-beaten mate, with the alacrity of a juggler, makes a long leg back to the cabin pannels at the same moment, and with his breast against the table, takes his own plate and the castors and one or two of the smaller dishes under his charge; and the steward if he can keep his legs, looks out for the vegetables, or if he falls, makes as wide a lap as possible to intercept the volant articles in their descent."

The monotony of our voyage, too, was sometimes broken by the appearance of an ice-berg, or a herd of black fish, porpoises &c. Or the Captain would speak a passing sail, or pay a visit to a neighbouring vessel, becalmed like ourselves. The ocean, likewise, in its roughest moods was grand, often splendid, and always beautiful about the sides of the ship on a cloudy night; the luminous phosphoric sheet produced by the friction of the vessel cutting through the waves being in appearance not unlike the milky-way in the heavens, bespangled, as it is, with stars, that sparkle and blaze along the side of the ship, and sail brilliantly away upon the dark blue of the ocean.

The first thing, says one, in his directions to a Steerage-passenger, is to be provided with the means necessary to pay the passage, and to get all your money in hand. Go and see the ship yourself. The taking of your passage must be a plain matter of business; the bargain made, the money paid, (about five pounds a head) and the transaction recorded in a written memorandum. Say others, you must provide your own bedding, see your biscuits and have them good, bring plenty of flour and fresh eggs, potatoes, butter, sugar, tea, coffee, oatmeal, patent groats, rice, salt, pepper, vinegar, port-wine, if you can get it, and a few simple medicines.

In addition to the preceding directions, I should recommend the Steerage-passenger to take his passage in one of the regular Line of Packets, as it will afford him the best security he can get, not only for sailing at the appointed time, but also for a safe and expeditious voyage : and if he has any regard for health and comfort in the steerage, by all possible means, and especially by a good example, let him promote cleanliness among the passengers.

The following verse which a celebrated traveller says carried him all over the world, I should strongly recommend to the consideration of Steerage-passengers generally.

I'll not willingly offend,
  Nor be easily offended ;
What's amiss I'll strive to mend,
  And endure what can't be mended.

For want of such a disposition I have known some very much displeased because they might not go to the water-barrels, lashed round the jolly-boat, and pump for themselves just when they pleased, but must be at the beck and call of the mate, obliged, perhaps, to take up their tin can early in the morning, while the sailors are swilling the decks, to receive their pint and a half for the day. And others I have seen, who verily thought they had got rid of all distinctions of rank and England together, exceedingly mortified to find a chalked line drawn across the ship by the mainmast, over which no Steerage-passengers might pass either on the starboard or larboard side of the vessel. In one instance, I was told, that the Steerage-passengers were so mortified by this same chalked line, that they drew another within a few inches on their own side of the vessel, insisting that no

Cabin-passenger should cross it; and being sixty or eighty able bodied men they carried their point. But such a disposition as this on board ship is as unreasonable as it is useless. After all they can do to make a Cabin-passenger comfortable, he is subject to sickness, confinement &c. equally with the rest, and surely he pays enough (thirty-five pounds) for the few conveniences which the cabin affords, and a slice of tough mutton &c., when he has the appetite to enjoy it.

If a man has any fear of God before his eyes, he will be more annoyed by the obscenity and profaneness on board, than by any thing else. It is common enough for the captain to give his orders with a curse, and for the sailor to growl out a curse in reply; and if the mates, stewards, cook, cabin-boy, crew, and some of the passengers be prophane, which is sometimes the case, a ship is little better thon a floating hell; and one scarcely knows which is more astonishing, the daring impiety of men amid the dangers of the seas, or the forbearance of a holy God.

Our captain, however, was not given to cursing, nor to speaking either. He minded his own business, and his stern forbidding aspect told other people to mind theirs; so that if a passenger asked him one question about the latitude, longitude &c. he seldom ventured another. He was a sober man, however, always on the look out, and very likely civil enough ashore. Indeed I don't know that he denied the

Steerage-passengers any thing reasonable: he allowed them even to perform worship in the steerage every sabbath-day, as there happened to be a minister on board. It is certain that he did'nt honour us with his company; and to speak the truth, the accommodations of the steerage were not very inviting. The preacher stood in the hatchway holding his bible in one hand; with the other he grasped a round of the ladder, to keep himself steady. The congregation, too, did not present a very orthodox appearance: some were ill in bed, others leaned over or lay along the provision boxes, and a few sat upright like rational beings; two or three rough sailors might be seen occasionally grinning down the hatchway; and altogether, many a worse excuse is made every Sabbath for neglecting Divine worship than might be found in the steerage of a Packet-Ship.

But whatever accidental or designed diversions there may be on board ship, it is a dull and tedious kind of life: and glad enough were all on board to see the Light-house of Neversink, on the night of Thursday the 3rd of May; and I question if the renowned Greeks cried the sea! the sea! with more enthusiasm than some of us shouted land! land!

The next morning we found ourselves sailing pleasantly up the bay of New York with Sandy Hook on one side of us and Long Island on the other. At five o'clock the pilot came on board. At six the news-boat arrived. About ten the

doctor reviewed us, and being all well, at five
o'clock in the afternoon, we landed in the New
World. The Steerage-passengers then separat-
ing, many of them for ever, made the best of
their way to boarding houses, and feasted upon
a fresh meal with a relish peculiar to people
whose staff of life for five weeks has been dry
biscuits. Very good accommodations may be
obtained at private boarding houses, amd also
at some respectable hotels, at the rate of a dollar
per day.

The next day we removed our boxes &c.
from the ship to the warehouse : and with respect to the Customs, a person who has landed at
both ports cannot but observe the difference
between New York and Liverpool. For example, I had about three hundred weight of
books, and before I landed them at New York,
the Custom-house Officer came on board and
glanced over the boxes with just as much regard
to one's feelings and convenience as the law
allows, (and *now* if the passenger will take the
trouble of getting a permit from the British
Consul at New York he may save himself the
vexation of opening his luggage at all ;) but at
Liverpool, I was put to the trouble and expence
of conveying them from the ship to the custom-
house, a distance of half a mile perhaps ; and
then, after waiting all day in the custom-house
yard, to save the officers the trouble of looking
over all my books, I was allowed the privilege of
making declaration before the proper authorites

that the books were all English; for which privilege I had to pay eighteen-pence.

New York has become so familiar to the people of England through the medium of journals &c. that I shall not detain the reader a moment by describing it. At the suggestion of some subscribers, however, who contemplate emigration, I will take this opportunity of inserting a table of American coins, premising that the value of foreign specie, as the English sovereign, the French five-franc-piece &c. is reckoned by the dollar.

GOLD PIECES.

The eagle . . value	10	dollars.
The half eagle. . .	5 „	„
The quarter eagle .	$2\frac{1}{2}$„	„

SILVER PIECES.

The dollar	100	cents
The half dollar . .	50 „	„
The quarter dollar . .	25 „	„
The shilling . . .	$12\frac{1}{2}$„	„

The sixpence.

The ten-cent piece.

The five-cent piece.

COPPER PIECES.

The cent . . .	100th of a dollar.
The half cent . .	200 „ „ „

Having converted our sovereigns into hard dollars, or bills current in the Western States, at the rate of four dollars and eighty cents to the sovereign, (more than we could get at some Exchange offices, and not so much perhaps as we might have got at others) the writer, with the family in whose company he was travelling, went on board a Steam-boat bound for Albany, on Wednesday, the 9th of May.

Every thing conspired to render the trip to Albany delightful. The excellent accommodations of the Steam-Packet, the rocks and mountains on either side of the noble Hudson, interspersed as they were with villages and farms, and gentlemen's seats glistering in the sun, formed a striking contrast indeed to the Steerage; and together with the extreme purity of the atmosphere, exhilarated one's spirits almost beyond bounds. The tow-boats, by which our luggage was conveyed, were lashed to either side of the steamer, and filled with Germans and Swiss, French, Welsh, Irish and English emigrants of the lower orders, dressed in their various costume. Whole families might be distinguished clustering together in this motley crowd; with their children and grand-children, gray-headed people after all their hardships at sea, about to form a short liv'd acquaintance with strangers, and then to lay their weary bones in a foreign soil. They appeared to be pretty cheerful however, in general; especially the young people, who often gave us specimens of their national airs; and particularly the Germans, who collected at the rising of the moon and sang for hours, with a taste and feeling far above the promise of a tow-boat.

On the Steam-boat, too, one evening, we had

C

a pretty good specimen of that fondness for debate so characteristic of Americans. The Captain of the vessel had collected around him a
number of passengers on the upper deck, whom
he had engaged in an argument respecting the
origin of human depravity; and was endeavouring very diligently to prove that every sin committed is the effect of example. About twelve
o'clock on Thursday night we arrived at Albany,
one hundred and fifty miles from New York:
the expense of the voyage for a cabin passage
was three dollars each, although on my return,
I paid but two dollars, and fifty cents for three
cwt. of luggage.

At Albany, the next morning, we removed our
luggage, or to use the American term, baggage,
at once from the Tow-boat to the Line-boat;
which saved us the trouble and expense of tak-
iug them to a warehouse. The distance from
Albany to Buffalo, by the canal, is three hundred and sixty miles; and on my return, with
excellent accommodations on board a boat of the
Trader's Line, the rate of *conveyance* for each
person, including his luggage, was one cent and
a half per mile, and of *board* four shillings of
American money per day. The Erie Canal
passes through some very flourishing towns, as
Troy, Schenectady, Utica, Rochester &c.; but
the scenery is as much inferior in point of picturesque beauty to that about English canals, as
the boats themselves, the appearance and behaviour of the captain &c. are superior. There

are some striking exceptions, however, to the dismal monotony of woods, that, for the most part, skirt either side of this great canal.

We passed the Cohos or Falls of the Mohawk river by night, and left the canal a few minutes, to gaze upon the moonlight splendour of the scene. By day, says Moore, "the fine rainbow which is continually forming and dissolving, as the spray rises into the light of the sun, is perhaps the most interesting beauty which these wonderful cataracts exhibit. There is a dreary and savage character in the country immediately about these Falls, which is much more in harmony with the wildness of such a scene, than the cultivated lands in the neighbourhood of Niagara. See the drawing of them in Mr. Welld's book. According to him, the perpendicular height of the Cohos Fall is 50 feet; but the Marquis de Chastellux makes it 76." The Genesee Falls at Rochester are not less worthy the attention of the traveller, but we must hasten on to the Great Falls, as they term Niagara, within a few miles of Buffalo.

On Friday the 18th of May, we arrived at Lockport; and from thence, instead of proceeding on to Buffalo by canal, we took the stage to Lewistown, seven miles distant from the Wonder of Wonders. The scenery was wood as usual varied occasionally by a tolerable farm with its frame or log-house, and that constant appendage a large orchard of apple and peach trees, at this season in full bloom. The stage-coach was by no means so comfortable as those we had been accustomed to in England, having a middle seat inside, the outside being wholly devoted to luggage. The road was pretty good, with the exception of a corduroy patch now and then, which gave us a hearty shaking. At Lewistown the roar of Niagara was not to be heard that evening, but it was distinctly audible during a shower of rain the next morning. About eight o'clock we crossed the river in a ferry-boat to Queenstown, Upper Canada, where we waited some time for the stage, ascending Brock's monument the mean while, and looking round upon the romantic scenery as far as a very wet and foggy day would allow us. About twelve o'clock we reached the Falls, and descending Table Rock by an inclosed spiral staircase, emerged at its base, where the whole sweep of Niagara poured down its floods before us with inconceivable sublimity. We had not the pleasure of seeing Niagara in smiles; instead of the rainbow

> " Brilliant as the chain of rings
> Round the neck of virgins hung."

the cataract was begirt with dense dripping vapours; and the spray which rolled up before us heavily soon mingled with the clouds, and was lost in the general gloom. But without attempting any description of Niagara myself I shall present the reader with that of Mr. Morse, which is by far the best I have met with.

"Niagara Falls are situated in that part of

the St. Lawrence which runs between lakes
Erie and Ontario, and is called Niagara river,
twenty-one miles from the former, and fifteen
from the latter. The water is precipitated over
an immense mass of limestone rock, which forms
the bed of the river. The width of the river in
a straight line, at the falls, is three-fourths of a
mile. But as its principal force is exerted in
the centre, the brow of the precipice has been
worn into the shape of a horse-shoe, and its
whole winding width is not less than a mile and
a half. This distance is divided by a small
woody island, called Goat-island, near the American side, which divides the cataract in two."
I would observe here that beyond Goat-island,
there is a narrow slip of land, (of which Mr.
Morse makes no mention) called Miss Iris's
island, as we were informed by the guide, from
the name of a young lady, who passing over the
swift current that interposes, first landed on it.
"The Table Rock is a part of the Canada
bank, which is on the margin of the great
sheet of falling water. It furnishes altogether
the most interesting view of the falls. The
eye, looking up the river, beholds it tumbling with strange magnificence over the ledges
of rocks, which, seen from this place, seem close
together, and appear to constitute a single broken
cataract. The immense mass of waters, greatly
increased, in its rapidity by this descent, and
perhaps still more by the contraction of the river,
rolls almost with an instantaneous motion to the

brow of the precipice, and shoots many yards beyond, as it falls over it into the abyss below. The depth of the precipice, the roar of the cataract, the mass of the waters, and above all, the inconceivable exertion of power, overwhelm the mind with emotions of sublimity and grandeur; and fill it with new and clearer views of the weakness and littleness of man.

From the surface of the stream beneath, there arises a thick and constant cloud of vapour, which mounts above the precipice to the height of more than a hundred feet. In clear weather, three primary rainbows are frequently visible at once in various parts of this cloud. These, when the sun is near the horizon, appear complete semicircles, and are often of singular lustre and beauty. Beneath the fall lies a thick mass of foam, which, for a great extent, covers the surface of the water. The whole perpendicular descent is a hundred and fifty-two feet. The depth of the river beneath the fall is probably far greater, for the tallest trees, descending perpendicularly, are lost for several minutes beneath the water before they re-appear. The banks of the river below are on both sides perpendicular, of solid rock, and of the same height with the fall. They continue of this height seven miles below Queenstown. Here the cataract is supposed to have commenced after the deluge, and from this place to have worn its way backward to its present spot. No one who examines the ground will doubt for a moment that this has been the case; and those who have lived for twenty years on the bank all attest this retrograde motion. These falls are in Lat. 43° N.

From the Great Falls we proceeded to Buffalo in the stage, crossing the river at Black Rock. At Buffalo we spent the Sabbath; and on Tuesday morning embarked in a Steam-boat for Cleaveland in Ohio. The distance is about 180 miles, and the expence of a cabin-passage is six dollars.

CHAPTER II.

"Are not these woods
More free from peril than the envious court!
Here feel we but the penalty of Adam,
The seasons' difference; as, the icy fang,
And churlish chiding of the winter's wind;
Which when it bites and blows upon my body,
Even till I shrink with cold, I smile, and say,—
This is no flattery."

"Oyo" appears to have been a sort of inter-jection among the Indians, and was applied to the river from which the State of Ohio was named by the earliest French travellers through mistake, the Indian name for that river being Kiskepeela sepe, or Eagle river.

The state of Ohio lies between 3° 32′ and 7° 43′ of West Long. and 38° 30′ and 42° of North Lat. It is bounded on the south by the Ohio river, which forms its limit for 466 miles; on the north by Lake Erie, which limits it for 200 miles, and the Mictrigan Territory; on the east by Pennsylvania; and on the west by Indiana.

In the year 1790, Ohio contained 3000 inhabitants, but such has been the rapid increase since that time by immigration, that its present population is estimated at 1, 300,000. It increased from 3000 to 55000 in ten years, and in the next ten years, to 409 per cent, whereas the average rate of the whole Union for the last ten has been but 33 per cent, and that of New England but a little less than 9. Ohio however contains 36,000 square miles, so that " yet there is room."

The seat of government is Columbus; and the most populous city in the state of Ohio is Cincinnati. The following is an estimate of the increase of population in Cincinnati since the year 1795.

In 1795	.	.	500	inhabitants.
„ 1800	.	.	750	,, ,, ,,
„ 1805	.	.	950	,, ,, ,,
„ 1810	.	.	2,320	,, ,, ,,
„ 1813	.	.	4,000	,, ,, ,,
„ 1820	.	.	10,000	,, ,, ,,
„ 1824	.	.	12,016	,, ,, ,,
„ 1826	.	.	16,230	,, ,, ,,
„ 1829	.	.	25,000	,, ,, ,,
„ 1830	.	.	27,000	,, ,, ,,
„ 1831	.	.	30,000	,, ,, ,,

Besides Cincinnati, might be mentioned as thriving towns in Ohio, Zanesville, and Circleville, Chillicothe, Steubenville, Canton, Marietta &c.

The uncultivated parts of Ohio in general are covered with the finest timber, but there are two species of natural meadow, called Prairies. " The name is derived from the early French travellers; who, in their own language, called them Prairies or meadows. They are clothed with tall grass and flowering plants in the spring, summer and autumnal months; and on the whole, produce an aspect, in those months, on a first view, very agreeable. It must be confessed, though, from their uniformity and sameness, having few or no hills in them, that their beauties soon become tiresome to the weary traveller, who traverses these plains; for such is their uniformity in appearance, that after riding all day across them, on looking around us at night, we fancy ourselves exactly where we started in the morning. From a careful examination of our prairies, wet and dry, I am satisfied that the dry ones are the more ancient of the two—that fires produced neither of them—that in their natural state, a luxuriant vegetation is raising their present surface every year; that the dry ones are extremely valuable for cultivation, and that the wet ones will, at no very distant day, furnish us with an abundance of fuel, in a country but thinly timbered, indeed almost destitute of wood, and without fossil coal, so common in our hilly region. If, as it is known to be the fact, our hilly region be well supplied with iron, stone, and other useful minerals, together with salt water, nature has supplied the same region wiih inexhaustible stores of coal, for their manufacture. If the level parts of this State, where the dry prairies abound, contain large tracts of rich land, the time is at hand, when they will be covered with well cultivated farms, where the rich harvests will wave, and where naturalized grasses will afford food for large flocks of domestic animals.

It is known that Ohio is wholly a secondary, diluvial or alluvial country. From the very nature of all secondary countries, there must be large tracts of alluvion. The streams have few rapids in them, are not very straight in their courses, are apt to overflow their banks, run slowly, and fail in the summer and autumnal months. The botany of such countries is rich, the water not very pure, and the air, at particular seasons, bad." Liver complaints are common in Ohio, and fevers and ague prevail very much in some parts at the fall of the year.

The Western Reserve is situated in the north-east quarter of Ohio, between Lake Erie on the North, and Pennsylvania on the east. It extends 120 miles from east to west, and upon an average 52 from north to south. The area is 3,000,000 of acres; of which 500,000, lying at its western extremity, were granted by the State of Connecticut as a donation to certain persons whose property was destroyed by fire during the revolutionary war. The manner in which the State of Connecticut became possessed of the said land was the following : King Charles the second of England, pursuing the example of his brother kings in granting to their subjects large tracts of land in newly discovered countries, conferred upon the colony of Connecticut, in 1662, a charter-right to all lands included within certain specified bounds. But the geography of America being very little understood by Europeans at that time, patents for land often interfered with each other; and after the United States became an independant nation, those interfering claims occasioned much collision between them and the State of Connecticut, which were finally compromised by the United States relinquishing their claim to the 3,000,000 of acres described ; *reserving* to themselves, however, the right of jurisdiction. Afterwards, this tract of land was united to the territory, now State of Ohio.

The most flourishing villages on the Western Reserve are Cleaveland and Norwalk, Hudson, Ravenna, Warren, Jefferson, Mecca, Elyria &c. To the surrounding country these villages answer the purpose of market-towns in England, nor indeed would be much unlike many of them in appearance, but for the foreign aspect of their numerous and elegant white frame-buildings.

At the mouths of the rivers, also, as the Rocky, Black, and Vermillion rivers, may be seen clusters of neat frame houses, answering to an English wharf. Where the river is provided with a pier at its junction with the lake, which is generally the case, it is a place of considerable business, emigrants and merchandize being landed there, and the various produce of the country shipped for Detroit or Buffalo ; from whence it is conveyed to different and distant parts of the Union.

Nor are there wanting along the public roads at convenient distances, the store or shop, the blacksmith's shed, and the tavern where travellers to the "far west" may find good accommodations, for man and beast.

In the New Settlements, generally, the houses are scattered over townships of about five miles square, after the manner of lodge-houses in the agricultural districts of England, every man's house standing on his own farm. But instead of the open country to which he has been accustomed, the Englishman feels as if he were imprisoned in woods. On either side of the road nothing is to be seen beyond the length of a single farm but woods! woods! Not like the groves and copses of his native land, rising from the banks of some meandering river, or crowning the top of some verdant hill, but, in consequence of the general flatness of the country, presenting to view a front row of trees only, relieved by the dark forest behind. In fact, it is emphatically a "wood country," for wood in the form of roads, or bridges, fences, houses, or barns, meets the eye at every point. By night, the traveller is lighted on his way with the blaze of huge piles, that crackling and roaring in the wind, irradiate the heavens; and by day the stroke of the axe, or the crash of the falling timber, is to be heard every where; while nothing is more common than to see several acres together strew'd with the loftiest trees, rank behid rank, like regiments of slain men; forcibly reminding one of the strik-

D

ing imagery by which the prophet Isaiah in the 10th chapter of his prophecies, and at the 33rd and 34th verses, predicts the destruction of the Assyrian army. "Behold, the Lord, the Lord of hosts, shall lop the bough with terror: and the high ones of stature shall be hewn down, and the haughty shall be humbled. And he shall cut down the thickets of the forest with iron, and Lebanon shall fall by a mighty one."

And if the stranger wishes to take a ride over one of these back-wood farms, thus shut in with forests, he will bear in mind that there is no *bridle road* in this part of the world; and instead of just putting forward the handle of his whip to pull open the gate, he will find it necessary to dismount, and lift out the bars from their mortices in the side-posts; aye, and to put them in again, too, before he resumes his seat on the saddle; or otherwise he may encounter the rebuke of yonder stern republican, who shouts to his dull oxen with the voice of a Stentor.

And after all the trouble of getting into these lots, as they term them, what a contrast to the beautiful and fragrant hedge rows of Old England do the bare zigzag wooden fences of Ohio present! And how disfigured its luxuriant crops by the half-burnt black stumps that show their unsightly heads in every part! Yet even these are not so alarming as the hollow trunks of trees through which the flames are still bursting; or, otherwise their black ruins present such dubious shapes to the lonely traveller, that it requires but a little superstition to convert them into fiends and hobgoblins, when the mists of evening gather across the road, and nothing is to be heard save the melancholy cry of Whip-poor-Will! Whip-poor-Will!

It is true, indeed, that the long lines of peach trees which skirt either side of the road appear beautiful in spring, dress'd out in their pink bloom; but generally speaking, the scenery of these New Settlements is monotonous and uninteresting to the lover of the mere picturesque.

There is one exception, however, that ought not in justice to be passed over without notice; I mean the Bottom Lands, or Flats, which accompany the several rivers in their course to the lake. These deep chasms appear to have been produced in the first instance by some powerful convulsion of nature, and afterwards to have been reduced to their present form by the ceaseless action of the stream. In some parts they fall more than a hundred feet below the common level of the country; in other's they descend so gradually to the water's edge as to admit of roads on either side, which are united by a bridge over the river in the midst. On an average these Bottom Lands are about half a mile in breadth, along which, and across which, the rivers wind their way towards the lake; here gliding in a smooth transparent sheet over their level pavements; and there foaming among the rocks or, bending gracefully and brilliantly from their upper beds, they plunge into the gulf below, and

are lost amidst the clouds of rising spray.
Sometimes, they wander among the mills, and
stores, and farms of a newly settled township;
and at others, they roll through the deep shades
and solitudes of the wilderness, where the bald
eagle scared in his haunts, " his sail-broad vans
he spreads for flight," and bears away.

The river Ohio itself, according to a certain
traveller, is accompanied with similar Bottom
Lands, excepting near its mouth and below the
Wabash.   The French call it, "The beautiful
river."   And the scenery along it is beautiful in
the highest degree.   It is bordered by beautiful
farms, to which industry is adding houses and
barns, orchards, and vineyards. Pleasant towns,
villas and villages appear, very frequently, as
you glide along this enchanting river. Cities,
with their tall and glittering spires; steam
vessels, with their dashing oars, leaving a
stream of dense smoke behind them, floating
horizontally along in the air, attended by a con-
vulsive swell in the water, snore or snort, as
they appear and disappear on the silvery surface
of the river."

That part of the Western Reserve lying
along the shore of Lake Erie, between the rivers
Cuyahoga to the east and Huron to the west,
may be termed a level country properly enough,
yet, strictly speaking, it is undulatory.   The
land rises gently from the lake into ridges along
which the inhabitants for the most part locate,
attracted by the conveniences of public roads

and good water: on these ridges too it is generally healthy.

If the houses on each side of these roads are a quarter of a mile apart, the road is called a street; and though the houses be scattered so thinly, that but two or three can be seen from any given point, it is called a town: we do not wonder, therefore, that to an American traveller, England should appear like "a scattered town," and pasing along our public roads like "travelling all day through one street."

The mail-coach roads on this part of the Reserve are certainly not Macadamized; but still with a couple, or as the Americans would say, with a good *span* of horses, vehicles of every description may get along very well during the greater part of the year. As a set off against bad roads, it ought to be mentioned, that there are no turnpikes to pay. Nor is there, at the entrance of their villages, any sign-board nailed up against the walls with such inscriptions as this upon them, "Beggars, Gipsies, and Trampers of every description, found in a state of vagrancy in this Parish, will be dealt with according to law." The traveller's feelings are not harrowed up at every turn by the sight of some squalid, ragged, wretched object in human shape. Indeed, during the whole two years of my residence in America, I saw but one beggar, andthat was a poor European, and I think, English emigrant, asking help by the way to her place of destination.

Many of the cross-roads in these New Settlements are bad all the year round, and the traveller may congratulate himself if he gets to his journey's end at all, though it be

"O'er bog and steep, through strait, rough, dense and rare."

At the corner of these roads may be seen in some instances a white painted hand-post directing "To the Lake," "To the North Ridge," "To the South Ridge" &c. In other cases, the traveller must enquire the way; and in his reply he may omit the "thank you Sir," for it is highly probable that this will be considered quite a work of supererogation, approaching nearer to the servile than the civil.

We cannot dismiss this chapter, however, without introducing the reader to one of those numerous farms, situated aside from the roads, in the very heart of the wilderness. The nature of the path to one of these lodge-houses will depend in a great measure upon the time that has elapsed since the house was built, and the farm cleared. At first, perhaps, the New Settler has no other hand-posts than hacked trees, or, he may steer his course by the sun. But, by degrees, the underwood is trodden down, and a track appears. In the fall, indeed, as they term autumn, the path is frequently covered with leaves, and with snow in winter, so that most of the first settlers have spent a night or two in the woods notwithstanding their yankee sagacity.

There is no danger from wild beasts on the

Reserve, for it is seldom that a rattle-snake is seen now, and bears are still more uncommon. Indeed, a summer's walk in these woods is sometimes very delightful. The wild flowers, it is true, are not very fragrant, nor are the birds very musical at present; but the grasshoppers' chirrup, and the loud tapping of the gaudy plumed woodpecker are always to be heard; and it is common enough to see a flock of wild turkeys, running away in the distance, or, if you come upon them suddenly, they will fly up into the trees and sit till you have passed by.

But, under other circumstances, a journey through the woods, even in summer, is by no means desirable; as will appear from the following extract from one of my letters home. "I have been down to the Lake Shore two or three times visiting a family that attend meeting here, and the first visit I made had nearly proved disastrous. The road lies entirely through woods, and it was with considerable difficulty by the track of horses, sometimes lost in brushwood, and sometimes in mud and water, that I groped my way out to the broad light, and fresh breeze of the Lake Shore. The sound of an axe however told me at some distance that I was approaching the habitable parts of the earth; and the musquitos, which haunted me like ghosts through the wood, like ghosts also disappeared with its shades, and I arrived in safety at the log-house of my good friend Mr. D. Now if you know any one who sighs with Burns for

> " A cave on some wild distant shore,
>   Where the winds howl to the waves dashing roar."

send him over here, and if he can make shift
with a log-hut,instead of a cave, why I'll warrant
him a situation to his mind.   Or if you know
any one who would rather with Cowper have

> " A lodge in some vast wilderness,
>   Some boundless contiguity of shade."

I can suit him to a hair.   But I must not for-
get my story.   This said log-house then, together with a frame one very near, are the only
houses on this part of the Lake Shore, the next
door neighbours, any way, being at least two
miles distant.   Notwithstanding the wildness of
their situation, however, and the rude appearance of their dwelling, Mr. and Mrs. D. are both
civilized and christianized beings; they are well
informed, and well behaved, and what is more,
they are members of the church in this place.
We had a good supper of fish, coffee &c., about
six o'clock, and they pressed me to spend the
night with them; but I had engaged to go to
Dover the next morning, and therefore could'nt
consent, although I perceived that a storm was
coming on, and that night was not far off; so
with Mr. D's horse and a great coat, I set out on
my way home.   I had not proceeded far, however, when the storm overtook me; and before
I had half cleared the woods, night closed in, and
I could no longer make out my way.   The fire-
flies indeed glanc'd athwart the gloom in every
direction, and the lightnings flashed through the

trees, but all in vain: I was lost. But if I was ost, I soon perceived that my horse was not; so I gave him the rein, and committed myself to the guidance of a brute, well assured that if he did'nt pilot me out of the woods I must stay in all night, wild a night as it was, for the thunder roared tremendously, and the rain poured down in torrents. Never, before, did I feel so much dependance upon a beast, and never, before, did I admire so much the goodness of the Creator as manifested by the instinct of dumb animals. On he went, slowly and cautiously, every now and then sinking up to his knees in mud and mire. Sometimes he would break his way through the brushwood to avoid the worst part of the road, leaving the rider to take care of himself by warding off the branches and young trees with his umbrella. At other times, he would stop short for a hint from the bridle as to which of two or three turnings from the more direct, but now almost impassable road, he should take ; but seeing that he was left to his own discretion, on he went again, as if proud of the confidence reposed in him, and at length brought me out safe and sound to the house of his master's brother."

As to the lodge-houses themselves, some of them are situated unpleasantly enough, and the following description by a friend of mine now resident in America, will serve for an example.

"Mr.— has raised his log-house on a churly, stubborn, clay soil, thickly covered with large shapeless stones, too hard to cut, and too heavy to move. He can get good wheat, I admit, and where his land is not covered with stones, it bears good grass. But there is no *road* to his house, for to call a stony, stumpy, muddy lane a *road*, would be ridiculous. You might get to his house by a better way, to be sure, if you would take the trouble to pull down a zigzag fence or two; but,it requires a stout man to do this, for rails or rather *beams*, of which these fences are formed weigh a hundred weight apiece, at least. His garden, &c. are enclosed with such fences. He has a good frame barn; but only one place where he can get water, which he is obliged to draw from a well for his cattle, and also for the use of his family; and after all, it is far from being good. He has cleared about forty acres. He has sheep, cows, a yoke of oxen, a mare and colt, geese, &c: but he can see nobody, and nobody can see him; he is surrounded with his own high trees."

Other lodge-houses, in these New Settlements, are more pleasantly situated. Let us follow this athletic figure before us; he is a yankee farmer, lately "come on," as the phrase is, "from the East." See! how he stalks along in his white chip hat turned up behind, with his axe flung over his shoulder! One would think he had signed the Instrument of his country's independence with his own hand. Perhaps the reader would like to be introduced to this lord of the wilderness. Good morning Captain Strong,

I have the pleasure of introducing to you a friend of mine lately from England, a Mr. Johnson.

Capt. S. How do you do Mr. Johnson, your better acquaintance Sir. And what does Mr. Johnson think of our new world here? "There is very much land yet to be possessed," Sir, you see. I persume, if we should ascend some considerable height in a balloon, in looking down upon this part of Ohio, we could see little or nothing but woods. I was reading in our newspaper yesterday, Mr. Johnson, that Kepler believed the earth to be a real living animal, and the flux and reflux of the sea to to be merely the effect of its respiration. Now, Mr. Johnson, we back-woods men have some curious thoughts come into our heads at times, as well as those who live in cities; and I was thinking, just as you came up, that to carry out the idea, the woods of America ought to be the back of Kepler's huge beast, and our new settlements here a bare place or so where the hair was rubb'd off.

Mr. J. A very happy conclusion truly Captain! But Captain Strong, how do you manage to preserve such a flow of spirits in these solitary woods? have'nt you a good many privations and hardships?

Capt. S. Hardships! We know nothing of hardships now to what some of our neighbours did when they came on, twenty years ago. Poor widow Smith often tells, with tears in her eyes, how their first crops were devoured by wild

animals—how they fled from their farms during
the war, terrified at the Indian tomahawk and
scalping knife; and so forth, and so forth, Mr.
Johnson. It's laughable enough to hear how
some of them got along at the first settling of
the country, I can tell you. I have heard of a
family who had but one bowl, and but one spoon
which they used by turns. And yet, they say,
so rapidly did the spoon go round, that a looker-
on would have thought there were as many
spoons as mouths. But those times are gone by,
Mr. Johnson; and now we have our grist and
saw-mills, our furnaces, and forges, and stores,
and villages in abundance. Ohio is a rising
country, Mr. Johnson, there's no mistake about
that.

Mr. J. But where do you obtain labourers,
Captain Strong ?

Capt. S. That's the greatest difficulty we
have to contend with. In England you haven't
land enough to employ the capital and the labourers; but here, whatever capital we may
have, we cannot obtain labourers enough to cultivate the land. The low price of land in Ohio
is the cause, Mr. Johnson. Your farmers sometimes *fetch* their servants on with them, but
they are soon off to set up for themselves ; and
as to your labourers, they work for us until
they can buy land for themselves, and then it is
"Good bye to you." A numerous family is the
most profitable kind of cattle we can raise in
these woods, Mr. Johnson. Our young men are

not afraid of getting married, nor do our young women pine away into old-maidenhood.

Mr. J. But how is it, Captain Strong, that so many of our emigrants return to England, and others fill their letters with complaints?

Capt. S. As to that, Mr. Johnson, some of your country-men, as well as some of mine, are discontented every where. Others were disappointed in consequence of exaggerated accounts sent home. And others, again, have been very unlucky in taking fever and ague so soon after they came on. In certain cases, however, which I could mention, Mr. Johnson, they are more to be blamed than pitied, for settling in swampy places, which they knew to be unhealthy; but "hasting to be rich," as the Scripture says, "they fell into a snare." But just visit some of your countrymen who received assistance from their parishes in England to pay the passage over, and I guess you will conclude that if they don't like their change, they ought to, any how.

Mr. J. Possibly I may, Captain Strong. And is this the way to your log-house, Sir? This lofty grove of trees, and these natural gravel walks remind me of a nobleman's park in England.

Capt. S. I wonder if they do, Mr. Johnson! Ah well; we have no noblemen here, for as our Statute Book says "No title of nobility shall be granted in the United States." There are some European noblemen and princes residing among us, it is true; but I guess the respect they meet

with depends more upon their character than
their titles. If your noblemen were all like the
truly noble La Fayette, Mr. Johnson, we
should not wonder at their being allowed
so much influence in the parliament of England;
but since nature pays no respect to persons,
it is a mystery to us republicans, how you
can get along with hereditary peerage. And
as to their parks, why you see Sir, we have
pretty extensive parks here, and no stone walls
to keep us out; nor Game-laws to prohibit us
from shooting as many deer and wild turkeys as
we please, in our own lots, or out of them.

Mr. J. Why, Captain! your barn makes a
greater show than your house!

Capt. S. There's no mistake about that. We
have to provide a good frame barn for housing
our crops; and as to our log-houses, why we
don't calculate to live in them long. And after
all, Mr. Johnson, I take as much comfort in my
log-house here, as I did in a brick one before I
left New England. It is true the wind whistles
through a little upon us in winter, but a little
fresh air at home prevents us from taking cold
when we go abroad. And I guess Sir, that my
farm-yard is not so snug as an English farm-yard
from what your people tell us. But walk in Mr.
Johnson, our log-house is not like a nobleman's
seat, it is true, but you shall be right welcome
to the best entertainment it can afford. Mr.
Johnson, I'll make you acquainted with Mrs.

Strong. An Englishman, my dear; I know you will be pleased to see him.

Mrs. S. I wonder if you have brought an old-countryman to see us! Mr. Johnson you won't be surprised that I am pleased to see an Englishman, for my father is an Englishman, Sir, and I fancy there is some resemblance to my father in every Englishman I meet; and indeed it makes me feel good when they call to see us. Pray be seated, Mr. Johnson, we'll make you as comfortable as we can; although you have come on a very unfortunate day, for in these woods it is our custom to wash every Monday,—Samuel, come here sonny, and put away these things.—Be spry.

Sam. Yes ma'am.

Mr. J. I should think Mrs. Strong, as you appear to be in a delicate state of health, that you find it difficult to get through your work this hot weather.

Mrs. S. It is rather tedious, Mr. Johnson; but I have to do it, for we can't get hired help here as we could in *Conreticut;* and upon the whole, I get along much better than one could expect, although I am sometimes down sick.

Mr. J. I am glad to see that you have some little girls growing up to assist you.

Mrs. S. Yes, Sir; the eldest boys are to school in the day time, but morning and evening they help us already in doing the chores* and

* Chores; a corruption of the English word, char.

notions. And indeed, Mr. Johnson, I have not so much to do as some of my neighbours, who— But we must wish Mrs. Strong good morning, or she will forestal our next chapter.

CHAPTER III.

"Forth goes the woodman, leaving unconcern'd
The cheerful haunts of men, to wield the axe
And drive the wedge in yonder forest drear,
From morn to eve his solitary task.
Shaggy, and lean, and shrewd, with pointed ears,
And tail cropp'd short, half lurcher and half cur,
His dog attends him."

THE New Settlements of the Western Reserve, in general, would still present a very wild appearance to an Englishman; but the aspect of the country has undergone a marvellous change, within the memory of the first settlers. Among the few of these pioneers still living is the venerable Judge R. of Huron County, at whose house the writer resided several months.

About thirty years ago Judge R. made a contract with a certain company in the State of Connecticut, called the Fire-land Company, to survey into townships and smaller sections, a tract of land containing half a million of acres, which was granted by the State of Connecticut to certain of her inhabitants, whose houses and other property were destroyed by fire, during the revolutionary war, as stated in the commencement of the preceding chapter.

E 3

At that time, said the Judge, (I give the substance of his conversation) this country was an entire wilderness, occupied by the Red-men of the Forest, or native American Indians, there being not a white man's dwelling nearer than forty two miles. The account we had heard of the Indians, led us to regard them at first with a rather suspicious eye; nor did their appearance tend to reconcile us to their company, being tattooed and dressed out in a very wild and fanciful manner. Sometimes they would procure whiskey of the few white traders then in the country in exchange for their furs, skins, &c.; and when maddened with this noxious liquor, they would threaten us with "We kill and we scalp too," unless their demands were instantly complied with : otherwise in time of peace the Indian is truly hospitable; he will share with you his last pound of venison for board, and his only buffalo skin for a lodging. The women however are excessively filthy in cooking, and the men very fond of smoking tobacco, and the leaves of the sumach, kinne kennick, a tree very common in Ohio. Every Indian arrived at the age of manhood has his tobacco pouch, his pipe, and tobacco; and when he has leisure he smokes so much that he is perfectly saturated with the scent of tobacco and kinne kennick. When we commenced our surveying, continued the Judge, the mark of the axe was not to be seen in the forest; although we found some large trees which had been hacked down with the tomahawk, for the purpose of catching racoons, or procuring the honey deposited in them by the wild bee. We cut our road as we went, unless we happened to fall in with an Indian trail; pitched our tent every night in the woods; and by day lived upon the stock of provisions we brought with us; having no other music to our feasts than the Indian whoop or yell, the howling of the wolf, the hoot of the owl, and the croak of the raven and the bull-frog.

From the statements made to the writer by others of the earliest settlers in this country, it appears that during the last war with the British these New Settlements were kept in continual alarm by the Indians, who hovered round to take advantage of the victory which they expected the British would obtain over the Americans on Lake Erie. The battle I refer to, is thus described in Hinton's History of the United States. "By the exertions of Commodore Perry, an American squadron had been fitted out on Lake Erie, early in September 1813. It consisted of nine small vessels, in all carrying 54 guns. A British squadron had also been built and equipped, under the superintendance of Commodore Barclay. It consisted of six vessels, mounting 63 guns. Commodore Perry, immediately sailing, offered battle to his adversary, and on the 10th of September, the British Commander left the harbour of Malden to accept the offer. In a few hours the wind shifted giving the Americans the advantage. Perry, forming the line of battle, hoisted his flag, on which were inscribed the words of the dying Lawrence, 'Don't give up the ship.' Loud huzzas from all the vessels proclaimed the animation which this motto inspired. About noon the firing commenced; and after a short action two of the British vessels surrendered, and the rest of the American squadron now joining in battle the victory was complete." The firing in this action was listened to with intense anxiety by those of the New Settlers who lived within hearing, and glad enough were they, when the thunder of battle, dying away upon the ear, indicated the retiring of the British toward Canada. "But oh! it was an awful sight" said an old lady as she concluded her narrative, "it was an awful sight, Sir, to see the flesh of our own people sticking to the masts and rigging after the battle."

At the close of the last war the Indians entirely deserted the country, and from that period, the tide of emigration, both from Europe, and the eastern States of America, set in rapidly toward Ohio. In some parts of the Reserve, there are whole settlements of English, and Welsh, and Dutch, &c. but generally, European emigrants are scattered among the Americans, who form the great bulk of the population, and are principally natives of New England. Some of these New England people moved from the Eastern States for much the same reasons that the labouring classes emigrate from our own country. I was once conversing with a

farmer on the Reserve respecting the compara-
tive advantages of the several States of the
Union, for the labouring class of emigrants; and
in the course of that conversation, he told me,
that when his family were young, he left the
barren hills of Vermont, and set out with his
wife and children in quest of a better country:
and after travelling about the States for seven
years, settling and selling out, at last he pitched
upon the Western Reserve for his home; and,
said he, "The Western Reserve is the place
for a poor man, there's no mistake about that."
Other inhabitants of the Reserve were men of
property in the East, and removed to Ohio on
speculation. Of these speculators, some were
very successful: water privileges or other local
advantages attracting numerous emigrants, villages rapidly sprang into existence, and their
estates as rapidly increased in value. Others
were disappointed in their expectations; various
causes operating to prevent the settlement of
their townships: and after labouring fifteen or
twenty years in a new country, they have just
emerged from their log houses to inhabit brick
or frame ones.

It may surprise an Englishman, if he be
unacquainted with the American character, that
farmers who were well off in New England
should leave a comfortable home for the wild
woods of Ohio. The best explanation of this
fact may be furnished, perhaps, by a comparison
of the English and American character, given

in an American Publication, called the Biblical
Repository, although penned for another purpose.
" This is connected no doubt, with a great feature
of European character, which at once strikes
Americans, that all ranks and classes there have
a far *greater enjoyment of the present*, than
ourselves. Our national character, so far as we
have one, consists in a spirit of enterprise, excited by the desire of improving our condition.
It may be shortly styled *a love of gain*—gain
not only of wealth, but also of reputation, of
comfort, of happiness, gain of all that is supposed
to be desirable. Our enjoyment consists more
in the striving after this gain, in anticipation,
and in the very act of acquiring, theirs in possession and quiet fruition." Local attachments,
domestic comfort, and almost every kind of
present temporal happiness, in the English sense
of the term, give way to the love of gain.—
Unquestionably, this was the principle which
led many of the New Englanders to Ohio; and
certainly the organ of acquisitiveness must be
very prominent in the Yankee cranium, for I never
met with a farmer there, however long he had
been settled, or however comfortably, but would,
from this same love of gain, sell out and move
away.

Now when an agricultural emigrant with
his family lands at the mouth of either river on
the Reserve, the first thing he does is to apply
for work at the house of some fore-handed farmer,
as those are called who approach nearest in

circumstances to the gentlemen farmers of Old England. Accommodations will then be found for his family until he has determined the place of his settlement. In the mean while, he will procure abundant supplies for his family in pay for his labour; and unless some unforeseen calamity should occur, he will soon find that he is going a-head, as the phrase is, a stout active man receiving fifty cents and his board per day for wages: not always in cash it is true, but in what is as good as cash to emigrants at their first coming on to a new country, in tea, sugar, tobacco, &c. which he will obtain at the store on his employer's account; or in pork, flour, potatoes, &c. which he will procure of the farmer himself.

When the emigrant is able to purchase land, he applies to the landholder or his agent, and contracts with him for whatever quantity of *wild* land he may want, which he will obtain for two dollars, and upwards per acre; paying all or part in money down, or commencing on a credit of five or six years.

He then cuts his logs &c. for a house; and when every thing is ready, he sends round the township to inform the inhabitants of his intended *raising*. On the day appointed, the neighbours assemble, one and all, if necessary, to raise his log-house; and very willingly, too, if they think him a *clever* man, or a man of good character, a well meaning man, as we should say; every such New Settler among them being considered an acquisition. The logs being rolled or lifted up one upon another, which is done in a few hours, the New Settler is left to cover it in with pine shingles, and finish it off at his leisure, and according to his fancy.

Now with a house well fixed, and a good *title* to his land, for this ought to be carefully looked after, as a matter of primary importance, the emigrant may set to work with a cheerful heart, especially if he has some stout boys to help him. He must work, it is true, but he works for the first time on his own land; and every stroke of his axe tells to his own advantage, and to the benefit of his children and descendants.

"First of all, the underwood has all to be taken up by the root with a mattock: this is called grubbing. Every sapling less than four inches in diameter must be taken out, and piled up in heaps and burned. When this is done you commence cutting down the timber; the straightest of which after being cut down, is measured off in lengths of eleven feet, so far as the body of the tree will admit, and cut and split into rails of about four inches diameter, for the purpose of inclosures. All other timber is cut down and piled up in heaps, and burned, or hauled off the ground. You next commence building your fence, by laying three rails horizontally on the ground, with one end resting on the other, in a zigzag manner, forming obtuse angles. A good fence requires to be at least seven rails high. When this is done you may enter with the plough."

The above proceedings apply particularly to emigrants who land on the Reserve with little or no property. But some of the poorest choose at first to work on shares, taking a part of the crops they cultivate for others in pay for their own labour : or they rent cleared farms for a certain term of years, until they can purchase improved land for themselves, and thereby avoid the toil of felling trees, logging, &c. If an emigrant, intending to take up his residence as a farmer, bring on property, he may purchase the best of farms, in the best situations, according to his means. And if he be a smart man, and do not intend to take a farm, he may find ways and means to turn his capital to good account, as will appear from the following statements made by a friend of mine, now a resident of Cleaveland, Ohio, in one of his letters home. "I have left farming, finding that here a farmer must not only plough for, but sow, reap, mow, thrash, and then sell his crop or barter it away *himself*. It is not here, *you* do this or that, or *we* do it; but it is *I*, I must do it myself or it will go undone. I have bought a pretty house and building lot in Cleaveland, which has increased from 500 to 700 dollars in value since I purchased it last July. I bought a lot of land in July last for 300 dollars, and sold a small part of it immediately for 200 dollars. Two months after, the purchaser sold half that lot for 200 dollars, thus clearing his own. I sold another lot of it for 150 dollars, and have still two other lots equal to the latter, worth at least 300 dollars. Thus you will see 850 dollars have sprung from 300, and all since last July. If Mr. — had bought land when he first came into the country, to the amount of 30 dollars, in some parts of this village, the same land would now be worth 20,000 dollars ; and his farm has not increased in value, independently of improvements, above twenty per cent."

Openings for stores also are naturally created in the New Settlements by the rapid increase of a population, chiefly pursuing agriculture; but these openings, in general, are anticipated and filled up by their own shrewd merchants. Carpenters, however, and blacksmiths, masons, tailors, tanners, shoemakers, &c. are almost sure of employment; and are well paid for their work, although the English are apt to grumble because they cannot always get cash for their wages.

In many townships too, there is room for medical practitioners, all of whom are called *physicians*. I have an Advertisement now lying before me which I insert as a specimen.

———

A GOOD STAND FOR A PHYSICIAN.

———

The subscriber will relinquish the stand which he now occupies, for the practice of physic, at the centre of this township, in favour of any one who will purchase his property, situated within one-fourth of a mile of the centre aforesaid, and consisting of eighteen and a half acres of land, whereon is a convenient dwelling house, office, barn, &c. &c. Those wishing for such a stand are invited to call and examine for themselves,

J. LANE.

Nelson, Portage Co. Dec. 24th, 1833.

———

Law, also, is very cheap in Ohio; and lawsuits frequently occur among the New Settlers, without occasioning the slightest interruption in their apparent friendship. But as English physicians and counsellors might possibly object to receiving pork and potatoes &c. in payment of their services &c. &c., we shall proceed with the occupations of the farmer.

In the month of March, as soon as the sap begins to stir, the farmers on the Reserve who possess maple trees enough, and think it worth while, make their sugar for the year. The Sugar Bush is situated in the midst of the woods, or in a clearing, and occupies a space of any extent according to the number of maple trees, and the quantity of sugar wanted. From one hundred to three hundred trees are tapped by most families, being enough to furnish them with sugar for home consumption. The sugar-maple grows to the height of eighty feet, with a proportionate diameter. The trees are tapped by boring one or more holes, two or three feet from the ground, into which a pipe of elder or sumach is fixed, for the purpose of conveying the sap into troughs placed beneath. One tree will yield from five to fifteen gallons of sap per day, according to its size, the weather &c. If the wood trees are left in cleared land they will not yield so much; indeed, they seldom thrive under such circumstances, and sometimes die away as if they had been girdled, or cut round through the bark with an axe. On an average, one barrel of sap produces five pounds of sugar. The boiling apparatus is situated in the midst of the Sap Bush, and consists, generally, of two rough forked posts, firmly driven into the ground, with a cross-bar at top, from which are suspended the caldrons for boiling sap. As the troughs are filled, the sap is collected in pails, and emptied into the boilers. Some place a trough above, from which the sap runs gradually into the caldron by pipes. But necessity is the mother of invention, and I observed, in one instance, that an Englishman who had to conduct the sugaring alone, had fixed a long pole to the handle of each caldron, so poised, that as the caldron grew light by evaporation, the weight of the pole raised it from the fire, in the manner of a lever, the cross-bar serving for a fulcrum. By this simple contrivance he prevented the caldron from boiling over to much waste, while he was absent gathering sap. When the sap runs from the tree it is perfectly clear, and not to be distinguished from water but by the sweetness of its taste; in boiling, however, it assumes a

colour which deepens gradually until it is boiled
down to syrup, when it has much the appearance of molasses. The next process is to strain
it; after which it is cleansed, by being boiled
with milk and eggs, when the impurity rising in
scum is taken off, and the remainder cakes down
into sugar.

But now the pretty bluebird ushers in the
Spring; and his simple ditty is soon followed by
the croaking or rather whistling of frogs, in every
pool and puddle; the whining of the mosquitoe
in one's ear, too, convinces us feelingly that the
summer is not far off. By land, the migratory
pigeons sweep over the New Settlements in
flocks of a mile or more in length, flying so low
in many instances as to be easily knocked down
with a stick. And now the south wind has
cleared the lake, rivers, and canals of the winter's ice, and opened navigation. The waters
teem with every thing that floats, from the
magnificent Steamer laden with passengers to
the "far west," that dashes along the lake "with
a majesty and determination, which mock the
lazy or the fitful currents of the air above and
the deep below;" down to the humble canoe, in
which the schoolboy paddles himself across the
river.

Soon after the sugaring is over, in Spring,
the young people of this woodland country often
amuse themselves with fishing. Some try their
fortune with a net, or sein, as it is called there;
and others with a fishing spear, which is used

by night only, when the fisherman with a torch in his left hand, and a spear in his right, walks into the river, and attempts to pierce the fish that are attracted by the light; this he does pretty easily, the same light enabling the fisherman to see clearly, and dazzling the eyes of the fish. Sometimes, a great number of hickory-bark torches may be seen blazing along the river at once, eighty or a hundred feet below the road. The rivers on the Reserve yield a variety of fish as the sturgeon, catfish, billfish, pike, mullet, pumpkin-seed, &c. The most common, perhaps, is the catfish, which is large enough, with a due proportion of bread-stuffing, to serve a family of six or eight persons for dinner.

The month of May is the time for planting maize, Indian corn, or corn, as it is called in Ohio.

Among the most productive soils of the country for Indian corn, and indeed for most other crops, is the alluvial land on the Flats of the rivers, described in the foregoing chapter. With the comparatively negligent cultivation which they receive, these Flats will yield from 50 to 80 bushels of Indian corn to the acre; from 30 to 50 of wheat, from 50 to 60 of oats; about 30 of rye; and frequently from 100 to 150 of potatoes.

In preparing the soil for planting Indian corn, it is ploughed regularly over once, and then ridged by turning two furrows together, leaving the ridges four or five feet apart. Sometimes the corn is planted along these ridges in single seeds, about half a foot from each other; but generally, it is planted in hills, at right angles with the fore-mentioned ridges, so as to form rows both ways, for the purpose of ploughing between them when the corn is hoed, which is done twice during the season.

From four to five quarts of seed is sufficient to plant an acre of Indian corn; the stalks of which, when full grown, sometimes reach the height of ten feet; every stalk bearing from one to three ears; and each ear being from half a pound to a pound in weight.

Indian corn is cut in October, when from sixty to seventy hills of corn are set together in what is called a hock, or stack, four hills being bent down to one another, and twisted for the purpose of supporting the hock, which is tied round the top with a pumpkin-bine to keep it together. Pumpkin seeds are planted at the same time with the corn; and when the corn is ripe, the pumpkins lie scattered over the field, large enough, in some instances, to fill a bushel measure. Pumpkins are used for feeding cattle; or, they are cut up into slices, like peaches and apples, and then dried for winter's use. When stewed, they are used for making the renowned pumpkin-pie, so beloved by every true Yankee.

But to return. Sometimes the Indian corn is removed from the field to make way for sowing wheat &c.; and sometimes it is husked while standing; and the cattle are driven in to feed upon the stalks, which make excellent fodder.

Generally, however, the corn is left in hocks, to dry for four or five weeks, and then it is carried and husked. When husked it is put into cribs, or spread over the barn floor, until it is separated from the cob with the flail, or the hoofs of the ox which "treadeth out the corn."

The Indian corn is roasted or boiled when about half ripe in the month of August, and being well-seasoned with butter, pepper, and salt is a very favourite dish with the New Settlers. The Indians celebrate this first fruits, by the "Green-corn Dance," and give themselves up to feasting, &c. from which, and other customs of the Indians, some have endeavoured to prove that they are descended from the Jews.

After the corn has been ground, for which the miller takes a tenth, as of wheat, &c. it is made into puddings and cakes. Some families, that I am acquainted with, use it commonly for bread; and the Indians of the North-west Territory live upon it.

Until the Temperance Societies had shut up some of the distilleries, also, vast quantities of whiskey were made from the Indian corn, one bushel of corn producing three gallons of whiskey. And, finally, Indian corn is used for fattening pork and feeding cattle in general.

Besides Indian corn, and crops commonly raised in England, the farmers of Ohio often cultivate flax and hemp, which, together with the wool of a few sheep, (kept chiefly for their wool, as geese for their feathers,) furnish employment enough for their wives and daughters, if there be a loom in the house; otherwise, the ladies merely prepare the material for the Factory, and escape the toil of weaving.

The manner in which husbandry is carried on in these New Settlements, resembles that of our own country nearly as much as the difference of circumstances will admit. The New Settlers cannot pay that attention to the different breeds of cattle, &c. which is paid by large Capitalists in England, and consequently, had no other reason, arising from the nature of the grasses, &c. been assigned, we should not have been surprised to hear English farmers, settled in that country, say, that the cattle of Ohio are inferior to those of England. The New Settler too, having to perform most of the labour of his farm with his own hands, thinks it better to clear a good deal of land, and take advantage of the vegetable mould, than to cultivate a little, economically, by manuring &c. The question with him is not so much, What crop will tend most to preserve the fertility of the soil? but, What crop do I most need? and then, How can I obtain that crop with least labour? In these respects, settlers in a new country proceed on much the same plan as the *squatters*, people in America who take the liberty of settling on new lands without enquiring the price either of purchase or rent; and when they have obtained a few crops from one spot of virgin soil, move out to exhaust another.

The English labourer in Ohio will notice the use of the cradle, or bow'd scythe for mowing wheat, of the sledge for drawing wood, and of oxen for all agricultural purposes. The English traveller too, will miss the gleaners in harvest, and the shouts of the merry Harvest Home.

From the time of planting Indian corn the heat gradually increases, until the humming-bird from the south returns to feast upon the peach-blossoms, and honey-suckles, and wild-flowers of these New Settlements. It is the red-throated humming-bird, (the Trochilus colubris of Lin.) and the most beautiful of its species. Gold-green above, white beneath, with gold-red throat, and purple brown wings, about three inches long. Frequently has the soft hum of these charming little creatures under the window, led us to look out, and watch them hurrying from flower to flower, with their little bills extracting the sweets as they passed, supported in mid air the while by a motion of the wings almost imperceptible from its rapidity.

The heat still increases until the Thermometer stands at 92° in the shade. Day after day, the same bright sun and lofty arched heavens present themselves; and in addition to the common temperature, a blast of hot air occasionally flushing in his face reminds the traveller of the simoon. But now the moaning of the wind through the forest portends a storm. Dense volumes of vapour roll up from the lake, volume after volume, in rapid succession, spreading as

they rise, until the whole hemisphere is black
with thunder-clouds, that discharge themselves
over all the country.

In the course of half an hour, perhaps, the
sun shines forth again with renewed splendour,
and the traveller pursues his journey, listening
to the roar of the distant lake, or refreshing himself as he goes from the peach trees, whose
branches, burdened with rich fruit, break down
over the zigzag fences on either side of the
road.

When a new settler has built his log-house,
and cleared land enough for the supply of his
immediate wants, he plants an orchard; and so
plentiful are the apples and peaches in these
New Settlements, that it has become customary
to help one's self, without troubling the proprietor by asking leave. Nor are wild strawberries,
cranberries, whortleberries, hazel, hickory, or
walnuts, butter nuts, hops, &c. less plentiful in
some parts of the forest. The vines in other
parts mount up to the height of fifty or sixty
feet from the ground, and then winding over a
hickory branch, perhaps, hang in graceful fes-
toons from tree to tree covered with wild
grapes.

It is customary for the farmers to pick up a
few bushels of hickory and butter nuts in the
fall, to eat on winter nights; and sometimes
the children of one family will pick up fifty or
a hundred bushels during the season, which
they sell at the stores for fifty cents per bushel.

At this season of the year, also, the farmers
make their cider, which is the common beverage
of the country. If they have no mill of their
own they take their apples to the mill of some
fore-handed farmer in the neighbourhood, and
pay him one shilllng per barrel for the use of
his mill; and if they make more cider than is
necessary for home consumption, they sell it
for two dollars per barrel.

The apples that are not wanted for cider,
they prepare for sauces &c. Many an evening
in autumn, while the old farmer sits rocking
away in his arm chair, the rest of the family are
occupied around a candle, preparing apples for
drying. One is occupied in paring them, which
is sometimes done by a simple machine con-
trived for that purpose. The apple is fixed to a
fork connected with a handle, which is turned
by the left hand, while a knife or rather, scraper,
is applied to the revolving apple with the right.
And so rapidly are the apples pared in this manner, that one parer can keep half a dozen very
busy in quartering and coring. When the
apples are thus prepared, they string them and
hang them up before the fire to dry, or, otherwise, spread them out to the sun on boards.
When thoroughly dry, they are put into barrels,
and are always ready for sauces, pies &c., pre-
paratory to which, however, they are stewed in
water.

Such an evening as this we are sure would
not pass away among such a conversible people

as the Americans, without talking.   Unless
Uncle (as they call every old gentleman in these
New Settlements) has rocked himself to sleep
after his basin of milk, crumbed with apple-
pasty, he will have some chat with young Norman, who has come down from the Ridge, to
help husk Indian corn.

Uncle. Well, Norman, I guess you haven't
husked fifty bushels to-day.

Nor. Not much short Uncle: And no mistake.

Uncle. So you've got an old-country-man
come on to the Ridge, have you, Norman?

Nor. Yes Sir, and a likely man he is too.

Uncle. How? a likely man, did you say,
Norman? that's more than you or I can tell.   I
guess there was some cause for his leaving
home?

Nor. Perhaps there might, Uncle. And how
is it that these old-country people walk so
clumsily?

Uncle. Did you ever see the sole of an
Englishman's shoe, lad?

Nor. Why no; I guess, I never did.

Uncle. I thought not, or you would never
have asked such a foolish question.   Why lad,
their shoes are soled with iron and hobnails.
Why there's more iron in an Englishman's shoe,
lad, than in Ben Clark's log-house, for Ben tells
me there isn't so much as a nail about it.

Nor. I wonder if they wear so much iron in
their shoes, Uncle! And the new comer's woman
walks in pattens, they say.   I was going up the

road the other morning, after the rain, and puzzling myself to make out what animal it could be that had left his track in the mud; and at last I met Doctor Taylor, who laughed heartily at my mistake, and told me it was the print of Mrs. Thompson's patten-ring.

Uncle. Ah well; I guess, Norman, they're none the better for their finery. They find mighty fault with us for chawing, but we dont smoke so much as they do, any how. And they are almost frightened out of their senses when they come on to find us working with bare feet in hot weather, but they soon follow our example.—I wish these old-country people would bear in mind that they come here for their own benefit and not for ours, and that they must knuckle to us about manners and customs, and and not we to them. And after all, Norman, they know no more about handling an axe than a woodchuck. Why lad, if an Englishman has wit enough to hack a tree down, he is likely enough to get killed by running away just under it.

Nor. It's true, Uncle, "there is not among them any that can skill to hew timber like unto the Zidonians;" but they handle the spade and the shears better than we do, and no mistake, Uncle. And then they are dreadful good mowers, for—

Uncle. How? what is it? mowers did you say? Don't tell me about their mowing, boy! I never see an Englishman but what I think of

the red-coats. Not that I'm afraid of their
troubling us again, since we have whipped 'em
out of the country; no, no! they had too much
Perry in the last war, lad, to ask us for more.
But what do you know about the war boy? You
were in petticoats when the British cleared off.
Do you recollect, Norman, when your mother
used to stop your bawling by telling you to "Shut
up! or the red coats will have you?"

Nor. I guess I do, Uncle; but then the war
is all over now, and for my part I like the English very well.

Uncle. Heh lad! it's their ruddy lasses that
you like. I guess you're *sparking* it with the
new-comer's daughter, heh lad!—Ah! well: it's
no wonder that our Eastern lads should catch
what comes, for we have no servants to send
unto their country and their kindred to take a
wife for 'em.—And can you understand her
brogue, Norman? There was a Yorkshire-man
here t'other day, and I guess he had forgotten
all his English, or I never knew any, that's
sartain. But what signifies talking? Come,
youngsters, bring in the wood for morning, and
get to bed.

When the cold weather thoroughly sets in,
the herds of swine that have been ranging the
woods all the summer, feeding upon roots, nuts,
&c. can no longer procure subsistence, and come
grunting round the farm-yards for Indian corn,
and are easily secured. But, sometimes, the
farmer has a great deal of trouble, and is out

two or three days before he can find his pigs.
At last he discovers them grubbing up the snow;
and recognizing his mark, he drives them home,
shuts them up a few weeks to fatten on Indian
corn, kills them, and salts the pork for the use
of his family, and for sale.

The farmer, in these New Settlements, takes
advantage of the fine frosts of winter to draw
in his lumber and stones for building, his wood
for fuel, &c. which he does very easily on sleighs
or sledges, while the snow continues. So much
more easily can they travel by sledges than by
wheeled carriages, that it is no uncommon thing
for them to take off the wheels of their coaches,
and drive them upon sleighs, the horses having
a strap of bells hanging round their necks to
give warning of their approach. Sometimes,
however, the weather is so severe, that the farmer
has enough to do in taking care of his cattle,
aud supplying his kitchen fire.

At this season of the year, also, those who
are fond of shooting find deer enough about their
Indian corn fields; but, generally speaking, they
are too well satisfied with their smoaked pork
and squashes to take much trouble in procuring
venison.

According to Dr. Shaw, the Eastern mode
of hunting, is, by assembling great numbers of
people, and enclosing the creatures they hunt;
and a reference to this mode of hunting may be
found in Psalm xxii. 16. " For dogs have com-
passed me ; the assembly of the wicked have
enclosed me."

This mode of hunting has sometimes been adopted by the New Settlers on the shores of Lake Erie in Ohio, and was thus described to me by one of the hunters. Notice of the hunt being previously given, on the day appointed, three or four hundred men, some on foot and some on horseback, assembled from the neighbouring townships on a line of road fifteen or twenty miles in extent, and about seven miles from Lake Erie. Each man brought his rifle or his axe with provisions for two days. When the signal was given the march commenced: and order was preserved as much as the natural obstructions of the forest would admit, by means of captains appointed for this purpose, who were continually riding backwards and forwards along the line. The first day was pretty much occupied by preparing for the march; and being winter, the hunters slept at night round about large fires piled up in the woods. The next morning at day break they advanced towards the lake, driving the game before them, and gradually closing in, until they reached a small circular space on the Lake shore, known by the trees marked with an axe: here they halted; and by this time the hunters who set out with a considerable interval between each, formed a thick fence of rifles. Several kinds of animals were "enclosed," but chiefly deer, of which there were four or five hundred. Many had escaped during the night, and through the irregularities of the march; but most of them

G 3

alarmed by the night fires, the blowing of horns
and shells, the report of guns, &c. had made
their way to the lake shore, and were " encom-
passed." When they perceived their danger
the alarm was visible among them. Some
leaped from the bank which was fifteen feet
above the beach, and plunged into the water;
but, being shivered through with cold, they soon
returned, although to certain death. Others
boldly attempted to force their way through the
line, and were pierced with the bayonet. But
the greater part of them, as if stupified with fear,
trembling, awaited their doom. A signal being
given, the firing commenced, and in a few minutes they were all dispatched. The hunters
then divided the spoil and returned home.

With respect to markets for their produce,
the Ohio farmers dispose of a great deal by
bartering it away at stores for articles of dress,
furniture, &c. and the store keepers turn it into
money. Or otherwise, the farmers themselves
send it off from the mouths of the rivers by
Schooners, to the more populous parts of the
country. Those who live near the villages, also,
can get cash for their butter, eggs, &c. without
any difficulty.

The following table will give the reader a
general idea of prices in Ohio.

Beef and mutton, from 3 to 4 cents ℔ pound.

Pork	.	.	.	6	,,	,,	,,
Sugar	.	.	.	12	,,	,,	,,
Tea	.	.	.	75	,,	,,	,,
Tobacco	.	.	.	18	,,	,,	,,

Indian corn 4 shillings American money ℙ bushel.
Wheat   7   „   „   „   „   „
Barley   5   „   „   „   „   „
Oats   3 and sixpence   „   ,,   „
Hay from 8 to 10 dollars ℙ ton.

Hardware, crockery-ware, and all kinds of linen and woollen goods, are more expensive than in England.

The reader who contemplates emigration must not imagine that he shall find no taxes in Ohio. The following was the amount of taxes for 1832, in Lorain County, upon every hundred dollars valuation.

State and Canal purposes   .   .   35 cents.
County ditto .   .   .   .   25 „ „
School ditto   .   .   .   . 10 „ „
Road ditto   .   .   .   33 „ „

Notwithstanding these taxes, however, the English labourer when he has obtained a farm of his own, is more independent, and more respected than he would have been in England; he obtains a livelihood more easily while he lives, and at death he may bequeath his property to his children.

But I have been asked with much anxiety by some, whose friends have emigrated to America. "Supposing an emigrant should be unfortunate, and unable to support himself, will they afford him any relief?" To allay all such anxiety, I give the following extract from the laws of Ohio.

AN ACT FOR THE RELIEF OF THE POOR.

"Sect. 1. Be it enacted by the general Assembly of the State of Ohio, That the overseers of the poor in each and every township in this State, appointed agreeably to the provisions of a law, entitled 'an act to provide for the incorporation of townships,' shall have the care and management of all paupers within the limits of their respective townships.

"Sect. 2. That upon complaint being made to the overseers of the poor, that any inhabitant or inhabitants of the township, is or are in a suffering condition, and unable to support himself, herself, or themselves, it shall be the duty of such overseers of the poor, forthwith to acquaint the trustees of the township therewith, and if the said trustees or a majority of them upon enquiry, shall be of opinion, that the person or persons for whom support is required, ought to be relieved at the expense of the township, they shall immediately issue a warrant to the said overseers, directing them to take such person or persons under their care, and afford them such support as their circumstances may require, &c. &c."

So much for the laws upon this subject; and as to the fact, in one township, where I resided, the only person on the town was a disabled Scotchman, who boarded amongst the farmers, sometimes at one house, and sometimes at another. In another township, there was a Dutch family thrown on the town by fever, and, being very poor, they were provided with doctor and nurse, and in fact with every thing needful for them, until they recovered. In short, I am persuaded that the afflicted and unfortunate meet with as much kindness in the New Settlements of Ohio, as in any part of the world.

CHAPTER IV.

"His form robust, and of elastic tone,
  Proportion'd well, half muscle and half bone,
  Supplies with warm activity and force
  A mind well-lodg'd and masculine of course.
  Hence Liberty, sweet Liberty inspires
  And keeps alive his fierce but noble fires.
  Patient of constitutional controul,
  He bears it with meek manliness of soul :
  But, if Authority grow wanton, woe
  To him that treads upon his free-born toe :
  One step beyond the bound'ry of the laws
  Fires him at once in Freedom's glorious cause."

"In America," says Dr. Franklin, "the people do not enquire concerning a stranger, *What is he?* but, *What can he do?* If he has any useful art, he is welcome ; and if he exercises it, and behaves well, he will be respected by all that know him; but a man of quality, who on that account wants to live upon the public by some office or salary, will be despised and disregarded. The husbandman is in honour there, and even the mechanic, because their employments are useful. They are pleased with the observation of a negro, and frequently mention it, that Boccarorra (meaning the white man) make de black man workee, make de horse workee; make de ox workee, make ebry

ting workee; only de hog. He de hog, no
workee; he eat, he drink, he walk about, he go
to sleep when he please, he libb like a gentleman."

The same state of feeling still exists in the
New Settlements of Ohio, with regard to every
kind of useful employment, and the husbandman, especially, is still "in honour there."
Almost every man is a farmer and occasionally
labours on his own farm. The tailor or the
shoemaker who works from house to house in
his particular calling; the blacksmith, the miller,
the store and tavern keeper—all employ their
leisure time in clearing their land or cultivating
it. Nor are agricultural pursuits in Ohio
esteemed at all derogatory to any office or
profession whatever, civil or eclesiastic. The
doctor returns from his rounds through the dreary
miry forest, and having distributed the draughts
or the powders among his patients, takes off the
empty saddle bags from his weary jade, rubs
her down with his own hands, turns her out to
grass, and perhaps, feeds his pigs; and yet his
skill as a physician is not doubted on that account. Nor is the sentence of the magistrate or
'Squire, as they call him, esteemed less wise or
impartial, even by the losing party of his
wrangling disputants, because Cincinnatus-like,
he is called from the plough tail to the bench of
justice. The good people of Ohio never dream
either that the word of God is less worthy of
credit, because it is dispensed on the Sabbath-

day by a clergyman whom they have seen milking his cows, or driving his corn to mill during the week. Such things as these are not at all uncommon even in the villages of Ohio, and among the New Settlements they occur every day.

If any professional gentleman ,on reading the above, should feel disposed to compassionate the case of his brother physicians, clergymen, or magistrates of Ohio, on account of their being subject to such menial and degrading offices, we can assure him, in return for his kindness, that the state of society, which dictates his compassion, is not unfrequently pitied, as well as deprecated, by his brethren of the New Settlements. Such being the views and feelings of Americans, it is natural enough that travelling ladies and travelling gentlemen, who expected the touch of the hat at every post and pillar in America, feeling themselves exceedingly mortified and chagrined, should return to vent their spleen in some slanderous publication.

It is a common saying among the farmers of the Western Reserve, " If a man is good enough to work for me, he is good enough to eat with me." And, accordingly, every hired person, male or female, native or foreigner, whom they employ, " is treated as one of the family ;" not in the sense that promise is sometimes fulfilled to apprentices in England, but bona fide ; for they eat at the same table, and at the same time ; all fare alike, and all fare well.

In illustration of the 123rd Psalm, "Behold as the eyes of servants look unto the hands of their masters, and as the eyes of a maiden unto the hand of her mistress, &c." Pococke says, "that at a visit in Egypt .every thing is done with the greatest decency, and the most profound silence; the slaves or servants standing at the bottom of the room with their hands joined before them watching with the utmost attention every motion of their master, who commands them by signs." The passage is well illustrated also, every day in Old England, by the attention, and often, obsequiousness of servants. But the word *servant* is not so much as mentioned in Ohio, hired persons being called *helps;* and certainly very little light is thrown on the above text of scripture, by the motion of their eyes, whatever company may be present.

It happened once that I was placed in a very advantageous position for observing the difference between America and England in this respect, the two countries being represented in the farm-house, at which I resided, by a hired girl from each. The Yankee lass was the daughter of a small farmer in the neighbourhood, and the English girl was fresh from the Old-Country. When dinner was announced for the first time after the English girl was hired, the American representative took her seat at the table as a matter of course, but the English girl stood aloof until she was bidden; and when seated with the family she looked as we may suppose a poor

H

Israelite would look, who, having taken the highest room at a wedding, or the chief seat in a synagogue, sees a more honourable man coming in, and expects every moment to hear the authoritative rebuke, " Give this man place." If any thing was wanted during dinner, the English servant rose instantly, as if she wished to make amends for her misdemeanour in sitting down with the family by diligent attention to their wants ; but the American *help*, the mean while, was very busily *helping* herself. In short the one took full advantage of the privileges belonging to hired people in her native land, and made herself quite at home ; whilst the other was a stranger and a foreigner, and had not yet forgotten that she was once a servant.

It is frequently very difficult for those farmers, who have much cleared land, to obtain help enough in busy seasons, as there is no class of people in Ohio to be depended upon for permanent labourers ; there are no *roundsmen* standing at the corners of their streets all the day idle. To secure against the inconveniences resulting from a scarcity of labourers, some of the farmers take children of about six or seven years old as apprentices for a certain term of years. The apprentice is clothed, sent to school, and provided for until he is capable of working on the farm, when his master or boss, as they call him, is amply repaid. Poor Emigrants from Europe frequently dispose of their younger children by apprenticing them to farmers or mechanics, since no premium is required.

With respect to the education of children in general, the Legislators of Ohio have not been unmindful of these New Settlers in our world, as Bishop Butler beautifully represents them.— Among the laws relating to the incorporation of townships, the following provision is made for schools. " That the trustees are hereby authorized as soon as they think it necessary, to lay off their townships into convenient districts, and the same to alter or change from time to time as the interests of the citizens may require, for the purpose of establishing schools therein; and each school thus established in townships, shall be entitled to receive an equitable dividend of the profits arising from their reserved section according to the number of scholars, and in proportion to the time they have been taught, or gone to school, whether such scholars have gone to school within or without the said township; and to enable them to make an equal distribution, they shall require a certificate from their respective teachers, stating the time each scholar has been by him taught, together with such other evidence as they shall think necessary to enable him to ascertain the time that each scholar has been taught during the period for which such dividend or distribution shall be made."

If but half a dozen families settle in a township they build themselves a school-house in the centre. This School-house on the sabbath is used for religious worship; in the week it is occupied statedly for a school, and occasionally for all kinds of meetings. At the appointed times, for example, all the white male inhabitants of the townships, above the age of twenty-one, excepting foreigners not naturalized, meet at the School-house to elect their township, county, and state officers. In the School-house, too, at other times, the various societies formed for the promotion of temperance and religion hold their meetings. And on the 4th of July the township School-house thunders with republican invective against tyrants and tyranny throughout the world.

The teachers of District Schools are chosen by the township, and licensed by an examining committee appointed for the county. These Teachers are generally the sons and daughters of the most respectable farmers in the neighbourhood, the former of whom are employed in the winter and the latter in the summer months. During the time of teaching school they board among the inhabitants, and receive besides two or more dollars per week, part of which is paid out of the public money as the law directs. It is customary for those Teachers who are pious to commence and close their schools every day with prayer; and the neighbouring ministers occasionally visit the schools for the purpose of addressing the children, &c. a collection of school children in these thinly settled townships affording one of the most favourable opportunities for usefulness.

Passing along roads and amidst scenery that promise no better guides than wild beasts, or Indians at best, the traveller sometimes comes suddenly upon a neatly painted frame School-house, and on applying for direction is answered by a well dressed and well spoken young woman of eighteen or twenty years of age, who is none other than the School-teacher. If he enter the School-house, he will be pleased to see forty or fifty boys and girls between the age of five and ten, with their neat clothing and pretty little bare feet, diligently occupied in reading, writing &c. Should he wonder how so young a female manages to preserve the admirable subjection and order which prevails, I cannot tell him, unless the secret be contained in the reply of a little girl who was herself a scholar under similar circumstances. "Do the children mind their teacher my dear?" said her mother. "Oh yes!" she replied, "we mind her because we love her."

Sometimes young men in Ohio take a district-school for a year or two previous to the more regular study of law, medicine, or divinity; as it affords them not only a comfortable maintainance, but much leisure time to prepare for seminaries and colleges. Many gentlemen in America who were once but district-school teachers, are now enjoying all the honours of the State.

Besides District-schools, however, there are what would be called in England, Academies, in the villages of the Reserve, where the young people finish their education.　　　H 3

I had the pleasure of attending an Examination of the High-school at E. which contained about eighty students of both sexes, most of whom were above fourteen years of age, and many of them one and twenty. The school-house in which the examination took place was open to all, and was crowded with visitors from the neighbouring townships, the friends and *connexions*, as nearest relatives are termed, of the scholars.

The young gentlemen passed a very creditable examination in latin, greek, mathematics, &c.; and the young ladies in grammar, geography, chemistry, &c. The young ladies, too, were dressed uniformly for the occasion, every one wearing a black silk gown with a white handkerchief about her neck, her hair braided with a garden-herb called hemlock, and her left sleeve ornamented with a white bow.

The Examination continued two days. On the evening of the first day the young ladies read themes of their own composing in the Court-house of the village, before an assembly of perhaps three hundred people or more; and in the evening of the second day the young gentlemen delivered essays on various subjects; some of them in a style that gave promise of future eminence as public speakers. The exercises were enlivened at intervals by a tolerable band of music, and all together were novel and interesting.

The advantage of such public exercises to young men about to play their part in the world, as citizens of a free and rising Republic, will be evident to all; but such publicity for young ladies falls rather below the English standard. Nevertheless we can assure the reader that so far from being too forward at home, the fair sex of Ohio are retiring and rather reserved; there's an air about them which to an Englishman at first acquaintance seems to border on melancholy; owing perhaps in some measure to the solitary kind of life they lead. And so ridiculously particular are they to keep aloof from an indelicate idea, that several terms which Englishwomen use without any hesitation, they have stricken from their vocabulary, and in the face of Webster himself, their own celebrated Lexicographer, are gradually changing the English language.

But let us follow the visitors of this School Examination home to their farm houses in the woods; and if for want of helps it is sometimes *tough* for the farmers in these New Settlements, it is certainly not less *tedious* for their wives.— Besides working up the flax and the wool, soap, candles, sausages, and indeed almost every thing consumed in a farm-house is home manufacture. Man however is a social animal; and notwithstanding their numerous engagements to back the Apostle's exhortation "be keepers at home," the ladies often find time for visiting.

From the first settlement of the country, when there was but one family to half a dozen square miles of untrodden wilderness, the New Settlers were very glad to refresh their memories occasionally by ocular demonstration of the fact that there were other people in the world beside themselves; for "a man" was then "more precious than fine gold; even a man than the golden wedge of Ophir;" and they almost started like Robinson Crusoe, at the track of a human foot, or the sound of a human voice. It is true, their accommodations for visitors were not always very elegant. I recollect a good Englishman who settled on the Reserve eighteen years ago, telling me that when a neighbouring family came to visit him, he was obliged to enlarge his table by laying the door upon it.

And still the accommodations of log houses in general ill accord with that suavity of manners and genuine hospitality we sometimes find there. In common with all other houses in these New Settlements, they have no grates in their fireplaces, but raised hearths with dogs of iron, across which they throw their wood; for coal is not used on the Western Reserve, excepting in the villages. In common with other houses, they are furnished with rocking chairs also; and it is customary to fix their beds on the ground floor; but unfortunately the lowest kind of log-houses have one bed room only, and that serves for every purpose under the sun. Sometimes, indeed, they bake in a brick or stone oven out of doors; and not unfrequently during the hot weather they wash by the side of a creek under shade of the woods; but still to eat and sleep in the same room is common.

If a stranger calls to take supper, which is the third and last meal with Americans, the good woman of the house will "make ready quickly three measures of fine meal," if necessary, "and knead it, and make cakes upon the hearth," probably in a tin oven set down before the fire. She will then produce her clean white cloth and set out the table. One by one, around the sides of the tea table will come on the cups and saucers, in company with as many plates as guests, each plate containing a piece of apple and a piece of custard pasty. In the midst, peering proudly over all stands the tea-pot; and in its neighbourhood, sugar and milk to *season* the tea, and the jug of hot water to dilute it, lest it should make one nervous, I suppose.—— Not far off, on the said table, may be seen dried beef cut up into slices, a dish of nut-cakes, sauces, &c.

Now with all this variety the good woman will entertain a stranger. Not that the stranger will be expected to eat all that is put upon his plate, much less every thing that appears on the table; but if he behave himself well, and make no invidious comparisons between the style of living in Ohio and in England, or any other country, he will be welcome. Probably too the stranger will be asked to *tarry the night*, for he will be quite at liberty to occupy one of the beds below, on condition that he will allow the good man and woman of the house, with a child or two perhaps, to occupy the other at its feet.— And if he should comply with this invitation he will not be dismissed the next morning without a substantial breakfast of fried pork steaks, boiled potatoes, toast saturated with cream, coffee, &c. &c.

In many log-houses, being *well fixed*, the bed rooms below are partitioned off, and every thing is neat and comfortable; yet the accommodations are not to be compared with those of the frame, brick, and stone houses, which belong to the Gentility of these New Settlements.— Some of these houses are in external appearance equal to the best kind of farm-houses in England; although the farmers to whom they belong, in most cases, make their own brick, and perhaps assist the carpenter and joiner in the woodwork: for a Western Reserve farmer is not "a man with one idea;" nor is there capital or population enough in these backwoods to allow of much division of labour.

Nevertheless it strikes an Englishman that the internal accommodations of these houses, and the style of living in general among the Western Reserve farmers, is far behind the propriety of their language, the intelligence of their conversation, and the prevailing tone and cast of their behaviour. There is much to remind one of country-life in England two hundred years ago, as it is described in the following verses by the Lady of Colonel Hutchinson, Governor of Nottingham Castle.

> " This freedom in the countrie life is found,
>   Where innocence and safe delights abound :
>   Here man's a prince : his subjects ne'er repine,
>   When on his back their wealthy fleeces shine.
>   If for his appetite the fattest die,
>   Those who survive will rayse no mutinie :
>   His table is with home-gott dainties crown'd,
>   With friends, not flatterers, encompast round :
>   No spies nor traitors on his trencher waite,
>   Nor is his mirth confined to rules of state :
>   An armed guard he neither hath nor needs,
>   Nor fears a poyson'd morsell when he feeds :
>   Bright constellations hang above his head,
>   Beneath his feet are ffowrie carpetts spread :
>   The merrie birds delight him with their songs,
>   And healthful ayre his happie life prolongs.
>   In summer merrily his flocks he sheares,
>   And in cold weather their warm fleeces weares :
>   Unto his ease he fashions all his clothes :
>   His cup with uninfected liquor flows."

In winter the merry sleigh bells, clearly tinkling through the frosty air, announce a party of pleasure, sliding along the roads of beaten snow to spend *New-Year's,* or some occasional holiday. In the summer, it is common enough to see the farmers' wives and daughters, with their green-silk-calash bonnets trooping to a *Bee* as it is called, or an assembly of women summoned for the purpose of quilting, &c. perhaps to fit out some young damsel for her wedding-day.

By law any ordained minister of any religious society, who has obtained a license for that purpose, or any justice of the peace in his county may solemnize marriages. It is customary for persons to be married by a license, which is obtained from the clerk of common pleas for 75 cents; and for professors of religion to be married by their own pastors; to whom they sometimes make handsome presents, so that marriage fees are quite a consideration in the clergyman's income. According to the etiquette of the country the marriage takes place at the house of the bride; and the service is simple enough. The bride and bridegroom being ushered in by some friend take their station arm in arm before the priest. A suitable portion of Scripture is then read, and a short prayer offered; after which the minister makes what observation he pleases upon the institution of marriage, and causing the bridegroom and bride to join their hands, pronounces the marriage covenant, first to the man in these words; "You take this woman whom you hold by the hand to be your lawful and married wife, &c;" and then to the woman, "You take this man, &c." to which form of words both heartily assenting and consenting, they are pronounced man and wife, according to the ordinance of God and laws of their country. Another prayer for a blessing upon the union is then offered, and the serious part of the ceremony is concluded by singing a hymn.

The Clergyman having done his part to the satisfaction of all concerned, the young people begin theirs. Each young gentleman in his

turn takes a young lady by the hand and intro-
duces her to the blushing bride whom they both
salute with a kiss, congratulating the bridegroom
at the same time with suitable compliments and
shaking of hands.

But besides these occasional holidays, the 4th
of July, the Anniversary of American Independence, is celebrated with as much enthusiasm in
these New Settlements as it is in the proudest
cities of the Union.

If the reader wishes to see how the 4th of
July is celebrated in the American cities, he
may consult the work entitled " America and the
Americans;" the following extract from one of
my letters home will convey some idea of the
manner in which that day is spent in the thinly
settled townships on the Western Reserve.

" I understand that you had a kind of Jubilee
in July to celebrate the passing of your Reform
Bill; on the 4th of July also we had a holiday
in these woods to celebrate the Declaration of
American Independence. I had received an
invitation some weeks before to attend the Meetings at B. about ten miles from hence. Accordingly I set out on the morning of that proud day
solus; forded the Black river at the turn which
leads to A; and after travelling through woods
for about five miles, busily employed all the way
in beating off the blood-thirsty flies from my
horse's ears, and the musquitoes from my own,
I reached A.; a beautiful little hamlet, consisting of a tavern, store, school-house, and some

I

half dozen white frame dwelling houses, enclosing an area more like an English Village Green, than any thing I have seen in America. In the midst of this Green the Liberty Pole was erected already, surmounted with a blue pennon floating in the breeze. A booth also was set up, covered with green branches, under the shade of which the inhabitants of that neighbourhood who had not joined the 'Cold-water Society,' as they call it by way of contempt, were assembling to carouse, and speechify on the blessings of Liberty and Independence; in the evening, I met some of this fraternity reeling home as similar characters do from a Village feast in England. But I, though not a signed son of Temperance, passed through the Green towards A.; and descending a hill on the other side, out of which flows a stream of the purest water that never fails, crossed the creek at the bottom, and after a few more miles of wood, arrived at B. The Meeting House was already filled; and a young Republican was reading an Essay on Independence in which were some harsh invectives against the tyrant of Great Britain, &c., all which I had to bear alone, being the only Englishman present, I would observe here, that this annual repetition of injuries, sustained during the Revolutionary war, is too well calculated to keep alive the bitter feeling of Americans towards the British Government, and to kindle such a feeling in the minds of their youth; and on this account is to be lamented. "The remainder of the morning was occupied in addressing the Sabbath-school-children who were entertained after the morning services with buns and cold water. In the afternoon a Temperance Meeting was held, when several speeches were delivered, with abundance of sesquipedalia verba, and similies without end. As a specimen of their similies take the following. 'To what shall I liken intemperance ? It is like &c. &c. &c. It is like the great beast spoken of in Scripture, with this difference however, the followers of the beast wear the mark in their *foreheads*, but drunkards wear it in their *noses*.'"

In the villages on the Reserve the 4th of July is spent differently. It was a fine morning in the year 1833, when the country-people flocked into the village of Elyria to spend their favourite holiday. About ten o'clock a band of vocal and instrumental music, composed of young gentlemen adorned with blue ribbons, and young ladies whose hair was bedeck'd with herbs and garden flowers, passed in procession up the Village Square to the Court-House, playing and singing as they went.—The reader will bear in mind that there was no mob to stare at these ladies, they were surrounded with relatives and friends, and countrymen, all alive to the noble sentiments which the day inspired.

The exercises of the day were introduced with a suitable prayer, offered up by a clergyman of the Methodist Connexion; after which Judge Ely, the father of this thriving village,

who gave it the name Elyria, read, with due
reverence for so venerated an Instrument, the
celebrated Declaration of Independence, which
received the sanction of Congress on July 4th,
1776.

Were it not so long, I would insert the whole
of this Declaration, for the sake of those readers
who may never have seen it. I must be content,
however, with observing that after setting forth
a number of grievances, or to use its own language, "a history of repeated injuries and
usurpations, all having in direct object the
establishment of an absolute tyranny over these
States," as the causes which impelled the
American Colonies to throw off their allegiance
to the King of England, it concludes in this
solemn manner. "We therefore, the represen-
tatives of the United States of America, in
general congress assembled, appealing to the
Supreme Judge of the world for the rectitude of
our intentions, do, in the name and by the
authority of the good people of these Colonies,
solemnly publish and declare, that these United
Colonies are, and of right ought to be, Free and
Independent States; that they are absolved from
all allegiance to the British Crown, and that all
political connexion between them and the state
of Great Britain is, and ought to be, totally
dissolved; and that as Free and Independent
States, they have full power to levy war, conclude peace, contract alliances, establish com-
merce, and do all other acts and things which

independent states may of right do. And for the support of this declaration, with a firm reliance on the protection of Divine Providence, we mutually pledge to each other our lives, our fortunes, and our sacred honour."

After the reading of this Declaration, the band in the Gallery of the Court House struck up, and having performed for a few minutes to the admiration of the audience consisting perhaps of four hundred people, a debate commenced which continued all day, with an hour's intermission at noon.

The disputants were Clergymen, Attorneys, Physicians, &c. some of whom read their speeches, and others spoke extempore with great animation. But here as at all other public meetings in America, I observed that no mark of approbation or disapprobation was shown. To hiss, or clap, or stamp as we do in England, even at religious Meetings, is considered by the backwoodsmen as a semi-barbarous habit. Indeed I never attended but one meeting in America where any such expression of feeling was indulged, and that was a meeting of the Home Missionary Society, held at the Chatham Street Chapel, New York, when the soul stirring address of the Rev. A. Reed, one of the deputation from the Congregational Union, was received with enthusiastic cheering by an assembly of two thousand persons.

The *debate* was between the Immediate Abolitionists and the Advocates of the American

Colonization Society; and it afforded one a good opportunity for observing the state of feeling among the New Settlers with regard both to slavery and the free black population.

With respect to slavery, there was but one opinion. No attempt was made to palliate American slavery by contrasting it with slavery in the British Colonies, or by comparing the condition of slaves on some particular estates with that of parish apprentices, or paupers generally in England; no: from the day that slavery was introduced into the United States by the Colonists of Virginia, when they purchased the twenty Africans brought into James's river by a Dutch vessel in the year 1619, up to the time of the meeting, American slavery with all its aggravations was held up to execration and condemned.

With respect to the feeling manifested towards free blacks, the Advocates of the Colonization Society, the exclusive object of which is to colonize *with their consent*, the free coloured population of the United States, maintained, that while the Society was admirably fitted by its moral influence to produce the *voluntary* abolition of slavery, it promoted to a very great degree the happiness of the free blacks who emigrated to the flourishing Colony of Liberia, and tended equally to the welfare of their brethren in Africa. But nothing more disparaging to the free blacks of America escaped from the speakers than such expressions as these,

" There is a natural distinction between the white and coloured population of the United States which does not admit of amalgamation; there is an instinctive aversion to it, &c."

The Emigrant may assure himself that he shall not hear the " smack of the whip, and the responding cry of slaves" when he arrives in Ohio; for, says the Law, "There shall be neither slavery nor involuntary servitude in this State, otherwise than for the punishment of crimes, &c."

I wish I could quote the laws respecting free blacks in Ohio, with as much satisfaction; but unless the following section has been repealed of late, it remains a foul blot upon the Statute Book. " That no black or mulatto person shall hereafter be permitted to be sworn or give evidence in any court of record, or elsewhere, in this state, in any cause depending on matter of controversy, where either party of the same is a white person, or in any prosecution which shall be instituted in behalf of this State against any white person."

The existence of such a law as this indicates a state of feeling towards the free people of colour, for which no apology can be made; and which cannot but manifest itself in ways alike disgraceful to the white, and injurious to the black population. But still, we should recollect that *our* opinions of the coloured race are not formed by personal knowledge and daily intercourse. And to deny the occasional Revivals of Religion which have taken place in America, during the last century, to be the work of God's Spirit, because such laws are in existence, and because instances occur of white people refusing to eat and drink with the coloured man, &c., appears to me quite as unreasonable on our part, as it would be for Americans to disparage the English Revivals under Whitfield and Wesley, because slavery was sanctioned by the British Government at that time, or because similar indignities are still shown towards the labouring classes of our own country. It would be more to the purpose, if those persons who manifest no energy about religion, excepting when they endeavour to suppress the energies of others more alive to the cause of God, would prove that Christians in America who profess to have been converted at such revivals, are guilty of treating the black population with contempt; and even then, such Christians might not find it difficult, in return, to convict their accusers of sin, although converted according to the strictest rules of orthodoxy.

The Emigrant will recollect that notwithstanding by the Census of 1832, it appears there were 37,930 free coloured persons in Ohio, there are none in the New Settlements of the Western Reserve.

But to turn from the merry scenes of Ohio to mournful ones: in his official capacity the writer had frequent opportunities of observing the manner of burying the dead in these New Settlements, and the following narrative is presented as an example.

The first time I saw Euphemia S. was at her Uncle's in V. She was an interesting little girl, with as bright and intelligent an eye as ever beamed. For her age too, being only twelve years old the day she died, Euphemia had made considerable progress in her studies, and was not unacquainted with the geography of England. "I love to hear about England," she said, "for I have read so many pretty books that came from England." She referred to the Young Cottager, the Dairyman's Daughter, &c. which are favourite school books in the New Settlements of Ohio. Indeed the publications of Leigh Richmond, Mr. Burder, Rowland Hill, Mr. Jay, &c. have so endeared their names to the good people of Ohio, that to meet with a person who had but seen the faces of such eminent ministers of the gospel, seemed to gratify them like hearing from some esteemed friend.

I had no further opportunity of conversing with Euphemia before she died, nor did I see her again, except at meeting one Sabbath, when I was struck with her fixed attention to the subject of discourse. One night some few weeks after this, her Uncle came to announce her death, and to request my attendance at her funeral the next morning.

It is customary in these New Settlements to bury the dead within one or two days at furthest after the decease; and two or more neighbours always sit up the intervening night to watch by the corpse.

In company with some of her friends, on the morning of the day Euphemia was buried, I repaired to the house of mourning. It was a solitary farm-house situated on the Flats of the Vermillion river. The descent was precipitate, and the river difficult to be forded, being half covered with ice; the wind too was bitter cold; but Euphemia was beloved by all the neighbour-hood, and when we arrived, the house was full of mourners.

"I believe" said a respected Clergyman who knew her well, "I believe that Phemy was sanctified from her infancy." And although she was not wholly free from the faults and failings of early life, yet the grace of God appears to have been communicated to direct her infant mind, and influence her youthful heart to re-ligion. Euphemia loved her bible, and would never retire to bed without reading some portion of it. And if, as was sometimes the case, her mother wished her to omit reading, for want of time, she would beg that she might read a little; "Only a short Psalm, mother," she would say; a request that could scarcely be denied. Eu-phemia made a constant practice of private prayer also, and manifested much eagerness to attend the public services of religion, and earnest desires to improve the privileges of the Sabbath-school. Nothing that affected herself alone seemed to give her so much pain, as to see some of her schoolfellows at the week-day school trifling and playing while the Teacher was at prayer. Frequently did she talk to them on the sinfulness of such conduct, and try to impress their minds with the uncertainty of life, and the solemnites of death and judgment: and sometimes she would express herself about dying, as if she had a presentiment of her own departure. Euphemia was ill but a week before she died, and from the time she was taken she seemed to be conscious that her sickness was unto death, and expressed no desire nor expectation of recovery. "Do yon feel resigned, my dear?" said her mother to the dying child. "O yes mother," she replied "for God has done it." "Are you afraid to die Phemy?" asked the anxious parent. "No mother," she replied, "for I trust in Jesus." And these if I recollect rightly, were Euphemia's last words.

It is customary in Ohio for the funeral service to be performed in the house of the deceased, before the corpse is removed. This practice, although attended with some inconveniences, affords a valuable opportunity for directing the attention of those assembled to the solemn realities of a future state; as it would betray an insensibility which, perhaps, few attain, to trifle with death while a corpse is exposed before their eyes. And this opportunity is the more important, since many who will not attend a place of worship, make a point of being present at the funeral of a neighbour, as it is considered but a common mark of respect. The funeral service for poor Euphemia, however, was performed at the District School-house, two miles off, as it was situated but a little distance from the burial ground, and the people collected were more in number than could be accommodated at the house. A portion of scripture was read, and prayer was offered at the house, before the corpse was removed, by a Presbyterian clergyman present.

The procession then moved forward slowly and in silence; some on foot, others on horseback, or in waggons: a simple cavalcade indeed—

> No "well plum'd hearse comes nodding on,
> Stately and slow; and properly attended
> By the whole sable tribe, that painful watch
> The sick man's door, and live upon the dead,
> By letting out their persons by the hour
> To mimic sorrow, when the heart's not sad."

No: nor was the decent mourning attire of the bereaved, simple as it might appear, at all necessary to prove the bitter bursting sorrow of their hearts.

The Burial Ground was a small space, enclosed as usual, by zigzag wooden fences; and although but a few years had elapsed since this part of the country was first settled, there were not wanting the tombstone and the epitaph to tell that death had found his way into the recesses of this wilderness, and of the few human beings that inhabited it, had laid some prostrate in the dust.

Having reached the School-house, the coffin was set down upon a stand, at the door, whilst the service was conducted within. The School house was filled to overflowing with relatives and friends, together with about forty of Euphemia's schoolfellows, many of whom were deeply affected. And it was truly a solemn occasion; for Euphemia was learning her lessons but the week before, in the very same School-house, and now she lay at the door, a cold and silent corpse.

After service, the coffin lid being removed, they uncovered the face of the dead; and every one in passing looked for the last time on the dear countenance of a child, or a sister, a relative a friend, or a schoolfellow, before they followed her to the house appointed for all living. Previously to the lowering of the coffin into the grave, a hymn was sung; and while the grave was being filled up, and covered over with turf, all stood by in silence.

Thanks were then returned in behalf of the bereaved, to the friends and neighbours; who always assist at funerals without any other remuneration.

CHAPTER V.

———

" Hence with thy brew'd enchantments foul deceiver,
  Hast thou betray'd my credulous Innocence
  With visor'd falsehood, and base forgery,
  And would'st thou seek again to trap me here
  With lickerish baits fit to ensnare a brute?
  Were it a draught for Juno when she banquets,
  I would not taste thy treasonous offer."

As the Temperance Cause excites increasing
attention in England, I have wandered a little
from the woods, in this chapter, to give a con-
densed account of the origin, progress, and results
of the Temperance Society in America up to the
present time.

It is by the distillation of fermented liquors
that ardent spirits are obtained, and they receive
various names according to the nature of the
substance employed. Thus brandy is obtained
from wine, rum from the fermented juice of
sugar, whiskey and gin from the fermented in-
fusion of malt and grain. Now ardent spirits
consist almost entirely of three ingredients;
namely, water, pure spirits or *alcohol*, and a
little oil or resin, to which they owe their flavour

and colour. The proportion of alcohol in ardent spirits is 53. 37 per cent, or more than one half.

"The common opinion that the art of distillation had its origin in Arabia, rests, probably, on etymological evidence alone. The word *Kahel* or *Kohol*, as we pronounce it, in the eastern languages is applied to the *stibium* or powder of antimony, with which the females formerly painted the whole, or part, at least, of their faces, as we read of Jezebel in the book of Kings. It was probably the same substance now used by the eastern females to tinge the nails, eyelids, and lips, and called *henna* or *alhenna*: the syllable *al* in both instances being the article equivalent to the English *the*. By a metonomy similar to that we now use in calling the same substance *spirit*, the word *Kohol* appears to have been applied to the product of vinous fermentation when separated from other substances by distillation, in allusion to its supposed purity or state of high refinement."

It is said that ardent spirits were first applied to the purposes of common life by the labourers in the Hungarian mines. According to some writers, ardent spirits were introduced into England in the thirteenth century. Others date their introduction much later, and affirm that they were brought by some British soldiers who had served on the Continent. However this may be, for some time after their introduction into England, ardent spirits remained under the care of the Apothecary, and were dealt out as laudanum, arsenic, or prussic acid is now. But like other stimulants, an increase of quantity was found necessary to reproduce the original effects; and what was measured out in minims, came to be required in gills, pints, quarts, and gallons.

The consumption of ardent spirits in England was greatly increased, soon after their introduction, by an Act of Parliament passed for the encouragement of distillation. According to Smollet, such a shameful degree of profligacy prevailed, that the retailers of this poisonous compound, set up painted boards in public, inviting the people to be drunk for the small expense of a penny; assuring them they might be dead drunk for two-pence, and have straw to lie on till they recovered for nothing. The same Legislature which had passed an Act favouring the manufacture of ardent spirits was soon obliged to interfere for its restriction. Laws at different times have been enacted, and fines imposed, to prevent the progress of intemperance, by the excessive use or abuse of ardent spirits in England; but all to no purpose, for the inhabitants of the United Kingdom of Great Britain still consume forty millions of gallons every year.

But from the Old World, we must trace this evil to the New; and instead of giving statistical accounts, as I might, of the quantity of ardent spirits consumed, the yearly increase of consumption before the rise of Temperance Societies &c. the following Allegory will represent the destructive progress of Alcohol in the United States, with sufficient particularity perhaps; and for this purpose, I present it to the reader, abridged from the Original.

THE SORCERER.

Some time in the eighth century, the precise year is not known, Alcohol, the Sorcerer, was born. His parentage is rather obscure, and at this distance of time the name of his father cannot be discovered. But though his immediate father is unknown, yet there is good evidence of a near connexion between him and Beelzebub, one of the ministers of Lucifer, the prince of the powers of the air.

The country which gave birth to Alcohol was Arabia; but, whether it was Arabia Deserta, or Arabia Felix, history does not inform us; most probably, however, it was the former.

Alcohol was a promising youth, and it was expected that he would prove a blessing to mankind. But it soon appeared that he was of a very fiery and malicious disposition, flattering only to deceive, and alluring to betray.

There can be no doubt of Alcohol being a real Sorcerer, for he is now some hundred years of age, and, instead of manifesting any of those infirmities which come with length of years, he is actually more strong and vigorous than ever. Besides this, he is too dexterous a thief to be any thing less than a Sorcerer. It is not saying

too much to aver that he has stolen more money
from the United States than the entire sum paid
for the support of Government. Nay, so adroit
is he, that he has stolen away many a man's
brains. And what is very observable, when the
Sorcerer has stolen away any man's brains, the
man thinks himself wiser than before; and when
he has filched away all his money, he is, in his
own apprehension, richer by far than ever. In
addition to these exploits, also, Alcohol, to effect
his ends, assumes almost an infinite variety of
forms, dresses, complexions, and names; and
accommodates himself to every circumstance,
taste, disposition, and rank. If his intended
victim is wealthy and fashionable, he appears in
a rich suit of red and purple. Then he is known
as Mr. Brandy, and professes to be a physician
of eminence, cures indigestion, and loss of appetite, removes *ennui*, and promotes hospitality
and fine feeling.—If his victim be not so rich
and fashionable, then he assumes a different
dress and name, and is called Mr. Whiskey.—
Sometimes, he finds his way into company as
the renowned Mr. Gin, a gentleman from Hol-
land. On other occasions, he is introduced as a
Mr. Rum, from the West Indies, a gentleman of
large fortune and fine address. Where he finds
caution and fear, the Sorcerer works himself
into favour by assuming the demeanour of a
mild, sweet, and insinuating gentleman, perfectly inoffensive and agreeable. His name then is
Mr. Toddy. Of late years, however, he seldom

bears this name; for most people, and *ladies particularly*, have manifested a good deal of distrust as to his real character.—Therefore, as all rogues do, he has found it convenient to change his name, and he now calls himself Mr. Mint Julep, Mr. Cordial, or Mr. Whiskey Punch, according to the taste of those upon whom he has a design.

Passing through the United States, Alcohol came to a little place, situated among the hills, called the Village of Temperance, as flourishing, happy, and industrous a village as ever the sun shone upon. No sooner did the Sorcerer behold it than he determined to mar its beauty and destroy its peace.

To accomplish his purposes, he assumed one of his most specious disguises. His calls at the Village were, at first, not frequent, and he never intimated a desire to become a resident. By degrees he insinuated himself into the confidence of a few leading men in the place. And now some of the pious persons in the Village, seeing he was not that vagrant knave some had represented, opened unto him their doors, and introduced him to their families; always, however, with a word of private caution, not to suffer him to use any familiarity. By and bye, the Parson, hearing from the members of the church how peaceably Alcohol demeaned himself, and having in his pastoral visits frequently met with him, invited him to an interview at his own house. Alcohol cheerfully accepted this invitation, and by degrees, the good man was so much taken with the Sorcerer, that he could hardly think of spending a day without his company; and very frequently, after severe toil in the service of Immanuel, he has been known to call for the Sorcerer to cheer his weariness and invigorate his powers. Indeed, I have myself seen the Sorcerer at several ecclesiastical meetings, and have frequently heard one parson introduce him to another, and extol his virtues; and, on such occasions, I have thought his influence much greater than it should be, either for the peace or the purity of the church.

By and bye, a house was built for Alcohol, in the Village of Temperance, and one of the members of the church actually became his *Steward*.

Very soon after this, the inhabitants began to complain of hard times, high taxes, and the ruinous tariff. Fighting, gambling, betting, horse-racing, Sabbath breaking, swearing, and every named and nameless abomination are practiced there. Indeed, the Village of Temperance has been entirely ruined, and its name is now changed, being known as the Village of Dissipation. The Steward still continues in the service of the Sorcerer, and has amassed an extensive property. But of late, it has been whispered round, that a greater than the Sorcerer has cited the Steward to appear before him; and it is even said that God will judge him; and that the witnesses against him are his former neighbours and friends, and even one of his sons."

It was the ruinous consequences of ardent spirits, and their increasing consumption in the United States of America, that gave rise to Temperance Societies.

The first Temperance Society based on the principle of Total Abstinence, of which we have any certain information, was formed at Moreau, in the county of Saratoga, New York State. On the 13th of February, 1826, the American Temperance Society was formed, and the Hon. Marcus Morton was elected the first president.

Total Abstinence and *Voluntary Associations, united by a mutual pledge*, are the fundamental principles of this Society; and it commends itself to all by its freedom from sectarianism, and by its patriotic and benevolent objects.

The formation of numerous State, County, City, Village, Township, School-District, and Family Temperance Societies soon followed; and the pledge adopted by these Societies in general is the following.

Mutual Agreement.

We the subscribers, residing in the State of——, County of——, Town of——, believing that the drinking of ardent spirits is, for persons in health, not only unnecessary but injurious; and that its use is the cause of forming intemperate habits and appetites; and while it is continued the evils of intemperance can never be prevented; do therefore agree, that we will not, except as a medicine, in case of bodily infirmity, use distilled spirits ourselves, or procure them for the use of our families, or provide them for the entertainment of our friends, or for persons in our employment; and that in all suitable ways we will discountenance the use of them in the community."

The reader will perceive that the first fundamental principle of the American Temperance Society is *Total Abstinence*. The Americans think that so long as the moderate use of ardent spirits prevails, the evils of intemperance cannot be prevented; their object, consequently, is to break up the use of ardent spirits, as a beverage, altogether; and, as the first step towards accomplishing this object, they set an example of total abstinence.

But the advocates of Temperance Societies in America have other reasons for abandoning the moderate use of ardent spirits; as, for example, in the first place, they think that *the moderate use of ardent spirits as a common beverage is unnecessary and injurious.*

In support of this opinion, they quote the language of Physicians, Generals in the army, &c., of which, the following may serve for a specimen.

" A man in health has no more need of ar-

dent spirit than he has of prussic acid, or laudanum."—Prof. E.

"The effect of moderate daily use of ardent
spirit, is worse than occasional intoxication, with
intervals of total abstinence, for this reason;
when the use is daily, the stomach has not time
to recover its tone and healthy action; whereas,
in the other case, after three or four days, its
regular action and proper functions are restored."
Dr. H. T. J.

General Jackson was once asked if soldiers
needed ardent spirits. He remarked in reply,
that according to his observation, those soldiers
best performed arduous duty and endured excessive cold, who drank nothing but cold water.

But although the Advocates of temperance
in America do not despise good authorities
against the moderate use of ardent spirits, they
depend more upon facts for convincing their
hearers and readers that it is an unnecessary
and injurious habit.

Governor Cass, the Secretary of War, in an
address before the Temperance Society, said, "I
stand here a living monument of the utter use-
lessness of ardent spirits, having never tasted
them,—and yet I have endured my full proportion of fatigue and exposure, in peace and in
war."

It is a stubborn fact, too, which the New
Settlers on the Western Reserve sometimes
produce at their Temperance Meetings, when
they come forward in the presence of their neigh-

bours and declare that since they abandoned the use of ardent spirits, they do the toughest work of the farm, much more easily than they did before.

Such facts as the following, also, are not unfrequently read from the Newspapers at Temperance Meetings. "The ship Rome, Captain Samuel Lennedy of this port, performed her voyage from Calcutta, without the use of a drop of ardent spirits on board the ship, although she was on our coast in the most inclement part of the late severe winter. We are enabled to add that the brig Baltimore, Captain Henry Towne, has performed four voyages from this port to South America and back, and that no ardent spirits whatever have been used on board during the whole period; and that no crew ever performed their duty with more activity, cheerfulness and efficiency.

Salem Gazette.

The following document shall close the specimens of facts. It is an Abstract of the Accurate Record of Deaths by Cholera in the city of Albany, from the commencement to the cessation of the Daily Reports, in the summer of 1832; omitting all under the age of sixteen years.

Temperate . . . 140
Free drinkers . . . 55
Moderate drinkers . . 131
Strictly temperate . . . 5

By referring to the Particular Record of deaths, I find the following observations annexed to these five cases.

132. Male, aged twenty-three, native, respectable, drank no ardent spirits, cause of attack, eating two pine apples.

303. Male, aged forty-five, native, respectable, drank no ardent spirits, attacked slightly at first, having nearly recovered, afterwards relapsed by getting wet.

321. Female, aged fifty-five, native, excellent character, abstained entirely from ardent spirits, supposed cause of attack was eating stale and soured preserves on the day she was seized.

333. Male, aged thirty-four, native respectable, drank no ardent spirits, neglected diarrhœa.

328. Female, aged thirty-four, native, respectable, drank no ardent spirits.

Members of the Temperance Society, two.

The following is the particular statement concerning these two cases.

200. Male, aged forty-two, native, respectable, member of the Temperance Society, drank no ardent spirits, according to the testimony of his friends, much distressed with fear, often told his wife he should die of the cholera, lost his appetite for food through mental agitation, neglected diarrhœa.

276. Male, aged fifty, industrious, member of the Temperance Society, drank no ardent spirits, in ill health previous to attack, laboured hard, exerted himself after diarrhœa.

Idiot	1
Unknown . . .	2

The undersigned physicians, members of the Medical Staff, attached to the Board of Health, residing in the city of Albany, examined the preceding document of facts before its publication.

Jona Eights, M. D. Chairman of the Medical Staff.

William Bay.

C. D. Townsend, M. D.

Joel A. Wing.

Henry Greene.

J. James.

Peter Wendell.

Barent P. Staats, Health Officer.

Henry Bronson, attached to the north hospital.

But in support of total abstinence, American Advocates for Temperance Societies alledge that *the moderate use of ardent spirits is an expensive habit.* Not that necessary and wholesome beverages are to be abandoned because they are expensive, say they, but it appears to us unwise to pay dearly for a beverage that is unnecessary and injurious. " Many labouring men spend, on an average, twenty-five cents each day for ardent spirits. This for three hundred labouring days would be seventy-five dollars. Now let us see what could be purchased with this money, taking advantage of the best season of the year for laying in family supplies.

Two barrels superfine flour, at five dollars per barrel, is   .   .   10 dollars.

Brought forward . .	10	dollars.
Twenty bushels potatoes, at twenty-five cents per bushel, . .	5	,, ,,
One barrel pork . .	10	,, ,,
One ditto beef . . .	7	,, ,,
Two cords wood, at five dollars per cord	10	,, ,,
Forty-eight pounds of butter, at twelve and a half cents per pound	6	,, ,,
One hundred and fifty quarts of milk, at four cents per quart .	6	,, ,,
Fifty pounds of candles, at ten cents per pound . . .	5	,, ,,
One barrel of soap . .	3	,, ,,
Balance towards rent . .	13	,, ,,

Dollars. 75

How many families wanting such a list of supplies are miserable, that with it would be comfortable !

Further, Americans think that *the moderate use of ardent spirits is a dangerous habit.*

The habit of moderate drinking, they say, has been a principal cause of the wide spreading scourge of intemperance. All the drunkards which have lived, or do live, were once sober men—moderate drinkers—daily tipplers—occasionally intoxicated—downright sots. Temperate habitual drinkers are the real authors of all intemperance. If the former did not exist, the latter never could.

"A spider had prepared his web in one corner of my room with great care and skill, and having completed it in the most perfect manner, he retired into its darkest recesses to lie in wait for his prey. Soon, a little thoughtless fly became entangled in the net, and the spider warned by the struggles of the victim to obtain his freedom, leaving his hiding place turned one web around him, and retired upon some slight cause of alarm. By and bye, he again approached the fly, turned another web around him and retired. This was repeated several times, till the fly was fast bound and incapable of resistance, when the spider fell upon him and deprived him of life by sucking his life's blood. The thought occurred to me, while I was watching this process, that there was a striking analogy between this spider, his web, and the fly, and the vendor of ardent spirit, his shop, and his customers. The spirit vendor builds or hires his shop, fills it with barrels, decanters and glasses, all arranged in the order best calculated to allure attention and inflame the appetite; and then a sign varnished and gilded, 'waves in the wind,' or glitters on the front. He then takes his stand, and waits for the receipt of custom. Soon, some unsuspicious one approaches and enters. A glass of 'cordial' is poured out, drank, and payment is made. Thus the web is turned *once* round. By and bye, he comes again, and another web is turned, and then another, and another still. Now the victim may make an effort to escape, but in vain. The web is fixed—the fetters are strong—the appetite is confirmed. There is no hope. His life is given for a prey, and a great ransom cannot deliver him."

If ardent spirits were a necessary or wholesome beverage, says the Temperance Advocate, we could justify ourselves in using it, and pray that we might not abuse it. But believing as we do that ardent spirits are unnecessary and injurious, the moderate use of them is a risk to ourselves and our families, which we dare not run. It is true that God has prevented many moderate drinkers from sliding into intemperance, but we find no promise in Scripture of the grace of God to prevent men from falling into any sin, to which they unnecessarily expose themselves. Nay, we cannot have the face to pray that God would deliver us from evil, while we so heedlessly throw ourselves into temptation; for this, in our view of the subject, is presumption. Therefore, "touch not, taste not, handle not," is our motto.

Finally, being persuaded of the truth of the foregoing statements, the Americans conclude that for them to use ardent spirits at all would be *morally wrong ;* and, therefore, they abstain totally from the accursed thing, according to the first fundamental principle of the American Temperance Society.

The second great principle of the Society is that of *Voluntary Associations, united by a mutual pledge.*

L 3

"In the fourth year of James I, King of England, the year before the first permanent settlement in Virginia, a law was enacted, which declares that drunkenness was a loathsome and odious sin, 'and the foundation of many other enormous sins, as bloodshed, stabbing, murder, swearing, adultery, and the like, to the great dishonour of God, and of our nation; the overthrow of many good arts and manual trades; the disabling of diverse workmen, and the impoverishing of many good subjects, and abusively wasting the good things of God.' We may learn a very useful lesson from the above extract, viz: No laws, however severe, will be able to restrain any vice, unless public sentiment be correct in relation to that vice. Thus James, as well as his predecessors and successors, enacted laws against drunkenness. Our fathers brought those laws with them to this country, and even added to their penalties; but drunkenness and drunkards increased ten thousand fold. What is the reason? Because whilst they endeavoured to lop off the branches they suffered the root to remain, and it sent up luxuriant shoots; they began at the top instead of the bottom. The *drunkard* was punished, but the *moderate drinker* was suffered to go on till he became a drunkard."

It will be evident to the reader, from the above extract, that the American Temperance Advocates despair of preventing intemperance among their countrymen, until they can put down the habit of moderate drinking. If the moderate use of ardent spirits were not expensive, injurious and dangerous to themselves, yet, viewing this habit as the source of ruin to others, they would feel bound by common humanity to break it off, and use every proper means to persuade their friends, neighbours, and fellow citizens to follow their example. And the fact that no Society is formed to prevent the evils arising from the abuse of other intoxicating liquors, appears to them a strong argument for exerting themselves to the utmost in preventing the vice and misery resulting from the abuse of ardent spirits. They are too well acquainted with Scripture to suppose that Temperance Societies, as a mode or means of preventing intemperance, are prescribed by Divine authority, any more than other modern Societies, which have been formed for the promotion of religion and morality in the world; but they do suppose that the principle on which Temperance Societies are founded pervades the whole Bible, and is expressed in the second Great Commandment, " Thou shalt love thy neighbour as thyself;" and that Temperance Societies are but an additional means and a new method of acting out this great principle. They feel it their duty to prevent intemperance by the best possible means within their reach. Precept and example had been tried in vain; laws had been enacted, and penalties inflicted, to no purpose ; at length, they remembered their ancient maxim, " Union is strength." Voluntary

Associations had expelled one mighty foe from their coasts, and they resolved to try their strength upon another, and still more formidable enemy, even intemperance.

The other branch of the second great principle of the American Temperance Society relates to the *mutual pledge*.

On this subject it is argued that "if a man be temperate from principle, he is the one who can best afford to give his name to the pledge; for it only gives a *form* to an obligation already felt. The solemnity given by the signature to a duty already acknowledged, greatly strengthens his purpose. It gives prominence and importance to the subject, and keeps watchfulness always alive. In this respect, it has the same place with a profession of religion. Some say, " we can be Christians and not connect ourselves with the church—we live according to Christian principle, without the form." But who that has entered on the profession, has not felt, that the fact of his having (so to speak) come under bonds by that profession or covenant with the church—the fact that he is a sworn servant of Jesus Christ, braces his mind in view of duty, arms him with more resolution, and enables him to act with more promptness and decision. So we conceive it to be with the solemn signing of the pledge.

Besides this, an important check is derived from the fact that others are *knowing to the engagements made*.

In every honourable circle too, where it is known that he is a temperance member, care will be taken not to put him in a situation where he will be tempted to violate his engagements. The known fact that he is bound, will direct the course of conduct; while, on the other hand, the same company will not hesitate to offer and press strong drink upon the man who has come under no engagement. If we take the case of two young men just emerging into life in these two situations, we shall, at once, see the advantage he enjoys who signed the pledge, over him who has not, in a circle of young men of high and honourable feeling.

Another advantage the man who signs the pledge will derive, will be a quickened interest in the advance of temperance. Nothing like the interest was felt in removing the evils of intemperance, before as since, signing the temperance pledge. The signature proved like an enrolment in a military corps.

Such is the general strain of reasoning in support of the two fundamental principles of the American Temperance Society, viz., *Total Abstinence, and Voluntary Associations, united by a mutual pledge.* Other arguments are employed, which apply particularly to ladies. That it is the duty of ladies to join the Temperance Society it is said, appears from the following reasons, among many others that might be mentioned. Because they control the fashions of the day, and especially as it relates to the entertainment of company : because they can do more than men to prevent the formation of intemperate habits in the young : and because the heaviest calamities occasioned by intemperance fall on them.

But, notwithstanding all the arguments produced in support of Temperance Societies, many objections were made at their first institution. Argument, however, soon gave place to ridicule and nothing was to be heard among the jovial sons of Bacchus, but Cold-water men! Cold-water Society!

Every artifice also was tried to induce temperance members to violate their pledge. The Rev. Peter Jones, Indian Missionary, in speaking of the present state of morals among the Chippeway Indian tribes, states that "they abstain entirely from drinking ardent spirits, although frequently urged to do so by the wicked white people, who use every means in their power [to turn them again to their old crooked ways. When the Indians at Muncey Town became [Christians, a white man who used to sell the *firewaters* to them, for their furs and skins, was very angry because they would buy no more *firewaters* from him. He swore against the Methodist Missionaries, and said the Indians would not drink so long as the Missionaries were among them; but that as soon as the Indians were by themselves, he knew he could get them to drink. So when the Indians got alone by themselves, the *white heathen* went and placed a keg of whiskey by the side of an

Indian path, where he knew they would pass,
and then went and hid himself in the bushes, in
sight of it, that he might enjoy the pleasure of
seeing the poor Indians fall into the snare.
Presently four of them came along the path; and
the foremost Indian coming up to it, stopped
suddenly, and exclaimed, ' so the evil spirit (the
devil) is here.' The second came up, and said,
' yes, me smell him.' The third shook the keg
with his foot, and said, ' of a truth me hear him.'
The fourth Indian, passing by the keg, gave it
a kick with his foot, and away rolled the *firewaters*, tumbling down the hill, and the Indians
went on their way, like brave warriors after
overcoming their enemy; and the poor, disappointed, and sadly mortified white man, was
obliged to come and take up the keg, and convey it to his own home, where, I suppose, he and
his friends opened and let out the ' evil spirit,'
and swallowed him."

In short, when the Temperance Society in
America began to rise above contempt, the
strength and virulence of opposition seemed to
indicate an alarm among the powers of the air;
and, what Calvin says of the opposition manifested against the great Reformation of Religion
in his day, may be applied with equal propriety
to the opposition excited against the Temperance
Reformation in America. " When all things were
immerged in darkness, the prince of this world
amused and diverted himself with the generality
of mankind, and, like another Sardanapalus, gave

himself up to his ease and pleasures in perfect peace; for what could he do but amuse and divert himself, in the quiet and undisturbed possession of his Kingdom? But when the light shining from above dissipated a portion of his darkness, when that Mighty One alarmed and assaulted his kingdom, then he began to shake off his wonted torpor, and to hurry on his armour."

In spite of opposition, however, the Temperance Cause prevailed, and every drunkard that was reclaimed gave additional strength to the argument.

I might here produce numerous instances to show the beneficial effect of Temperance Societies in America upon individuals and families, but the limits of the work will not allow.

The following extract from the Connecticut Observer will show the effect of the Temperance Societies upon particular townships, in some instances.

"ONE TOWN PURIFIED.

" In the year 1828, there were within the limits of the town of Lyme, no less than twenty two licensed retailers of intoxicating liquors, all of whom sold what they could, and manufactured drunkards according to law. In that year the temperance reform commenced among us. And the number of these licensed drunkard-makers has been gradually falling off ever since. From

one January to another, when the licensing
Board have met, the change in public sentiment
respecting the rum traffic has been very apparent.
A year ago, but two applicants appeared before
the Board; and on Monday last when the Board
met again, no applicant appeared to claim the
usual license: so that now it is our happiness
to state, that in a portion of our country, twelve
miles by eight—constituting the largest town in
this State—there is not a single grog-shop."

From the Report of the Executive Committee of the New York State Temperance
Society, it appears that the whole increase of
members during the past year, in New York
State alone, was at least one hundred thousand;
and that one thousand four hundred and seventy
two persons abandoned the sale of ardent
spirits.

"In America, within the last six years,"
says Mr. Colton, "there have been formed six
thousand Temperance Societies, embracing one
million members; two thousand distilleries have
ceased; five thousand tradesmen have discon-
tinued dealing in ardent spirits; seven hundred
vessels sail from American ports without it; five
thousand of the intemperate have been reclaimed; and the influence of the Temperance
Reformation on the community for the improve-
ment of morals, and other beneficial respects, is
obvious and vast."

With respect to the New Settlements on the
Western Reserve, many buildings that were

M

formerly used as distilleries have been converted to other purposes; numbers have given up the sale of ardent spirits; and the inhabitants in general, who have much regard to their reputation for religion or morality, practise total abstinence. The Temperance Society in these New Settlements, is esteemed as a handmaid to religion; and in some instances its introduction has been speedily followed by revivals. Temperance Agents come on from the East, and lecture in their villages; frequent and animated Temperance Meetings are held in their townships; Temperance Records, Reports, Tracts, Almanacks, Newspapers, and Magazines, are to be met with every where, and opposition appears to be dying away. The traveller will sometimes apologize for taking a glass of spirits at the bar of a Steam-boat, or Tavern; or if he sends for his whiskey to drink at home, he will tie a handkerchief round the jug; and when he is visited by members of the Temperance Society, he takes care to keep ardent spirits out of sight; unless he wishes to insult them, in which case, the first thing he does, is to set the whiskey-bottle before them.

But still there are Settlements on the Western Reserve, upon which the Temperance Societies have made little impression at present; such a Settlement I shall describe at the close of the next chapter.

And even where the Temperance Reformation has prevailed, the struggle between consci-

ence on the one hand, and appetite, obstinacy,
&c. on the other, was violent and long. When
the Society was first introduced, some rashly
declared that they would never join it, and
although they came as near to it as they possibly
could, by practising total abstinence, attending
Temperance Meetings, &c. yet they never could
be prevailed upon to retract. Many professing
Christians, for years after the introduction of
Temperance Societies among them, continued
to indulge themselves moderately with their
beloved *bitters,* or rather as Robert Hall termed
it, with "liquid fire, and distilled damnation,"
until, at last, they yielded to force of public
sentiment, although it subjected them to the
necessity of obeying their Master's reiterated
command, "Deny thyself." And ministers of
the gospel, who in some few instances manifested
a backwardness with respect to the Cause at
first, seeing its beneficial effects as auxiliary to
religion, became its zealous advocates; and to
their testimony against intemperance as Ministers of the gospel, added the weight of their
public protest as Members of the Temperance
Society.

CHAPTER VI.

"Yes in all lands
From pole to pole, or civilized or rude,
People there are, to whom the Sabbath morn
Dawns, shedding dews into their drooping hearts:
Yes, far beyond the high-heaved western wave,
Amid Columbia's wildernesses vast,
The words which God in thunder from the Mount
Of Sinai spake, are heard, and are obeyed."

THE restless and enterprising temperament
of Americans appears not less conspicuously in
religion, than in politics and the pursuit of private happiness. Under the direction of God's
Spirit, it maintains a perpetual succession of
Revivals at home, and sends forth a host of
Missionaries to preach the gospel in foreign
climes; but, accompanied with a weak understanding, and led astray by erroneous religious
notions, it vents itself in the wildest fanaticism.

One of the most remarkable instances of
credulity and fanaticism existing at the present
time in the United States is exhibited in Mormonism.

It appears that A. D. 1830, an Angel of
the Lord, as the Mormons say, appeared to a
certain individual commonly called Joe Smith,

at that time residing in Manchester Township, Ontario County, New York State, and discovered to him a number of plates which had been hidden for ages in the side of a hill at Manchester. On these plates was engraven the religion of Mormon in unknown characters, which characters Mr. Smith by a miraculous gift of interpretation, translated into English; and this translation constitutes the "Book of Mormon," otherwise called "The Golden Bible."

Hearing a good deal about this said Mormonism, I had some curiosity to see the Golden Bible; and at last my curiosity was gratified by a Mormon Elder, who brought me the Mormon Bible, and the Mormon Newspaper; and, besides, gave me some authentic information respecting this new sect.

The Book of Mormon is about the size of the New Testament, the peculiar phraseology of which is imitated; I suppose, to give the book an air of authenticity. The contents of the book are set forth in the title page as follows.—
"Wherefore it is an abridgement of the Record of the people of Nephi; and also of the Lamanites; written to the Lamanites, which are a remnant of the house of Israel; and also to Jew and Gentile; written by way of commandment, and also by the spirit of prophecy and of Revelation. Written, and sealed up, and hid up unto the Lord, that they might not be destroyed; to come forth by the gift and power of God unto the interpretation thereof; sealed by the hand

of Moroni, and hid up unto the Lord to come
forth in due time by way of Gentile; the interpretation thereof by the gift of God; an
abridgement taken from the book of Ether.
Also, which is a Record of the people of Jared,
which were scattered at the time the Lord con-
founded the language of the people when they
were building a tower to get to heaven : which
is to show unto the remnant of the house of
Israel how great things the Lord hath done for
their fathers; and that they may know the
Covenants of the Lord that they are not cast off
for ever, and also to the convincing of Jew and
Gentile that Jesus is the Christ, the Eternal
God, manifesting himself to all nations. And
now if there be a fault it be the mistake of man,
wherefore condemn not the things of God, that
ye may be found spotless at the judgment seat
of Christ. "

Such are the subjects concerning which the
book treats; and that the plates referred to
above actually were discovered, we have the
testimony of eleven witnesses at the end, pre-
faced by the following words; " Be it known
unto all nations, kindreds, tongues, and people,
unto whom this work shall come, that Joseph
Smith, Junior, the author and proprietor of this
work, has shewn unto us the plates of which
hath been spoken, which have the appearance of
gold; and as many of the leaves as the said Smith
has translated, we did handle with our hands;
and we also saw the engravings thereon, all of

which has the appearance of ancient work, and curious workmanship. And this we bear record with words of soberness, that the said Smith hath shewn unto us, for we have seen and hefted, and know of a surety, that the said Smith has got the plates of which we have spoken. And we give our names to the world, to witness unto the world that which we have seen; and we lie not, God bearing witness of it.

> Christian Whitmer.
> Jacob Whitmer.
> Peter Whitmer, Jun.
> John Whitmer.
> Hiram Page.
> Joseph Smith, Sen.
> Hiram Smith.
> Samuel H. Smith.
> Oliver Cowdry.
> David Whitmer.
> Martin Harris.

The Mormons have their High-Priests, Elders, Bishops, and Deacons, all of whom they send out by twos under the name of "Disciples," without scrip or purse; the families of these "disciples" in the mean while are supported at home, by the voluntary contributions of the Church. They baptize by immersion, on a profession of faith; and administer the Lord's Supper once a fortnight, or oftener, according to circumstances.

In their creed the reader will recognize the sentiments of certain English and Scotch fanatics of the present day; for every believer, according to the Mormons, possesses supernatural powers. In proof of this, the Mormon Elder with whom I debated upon the point, brought forward such passages as these; "If ye have faith as a grain of mustard seed, ye shall say to this mountain, &c." "And these signs shall follow them that believe, &c."

In reply to my arguments showing that miraculous powers were confined to the first age of the church, he observed, it is not said in the New Testament when miracles should cease, or that they should cease at all.

If every believer has the power of working miracles, I asked, how was it that Baxter, Whitfield, and Watts, and others, wrought no miracles? Because, he answered, they did not believe that they possessed the power.

To settle the point in a more summary manner, therefore, I requested him to shew me a sign. In reply, he told me that he lay two or three months at the Mouth of—— River, sick of a fever; that the skill of all the physicians in the neighbourhood had failed to relieve his malady, and at last he sent for an Elder of the Mormon Church. The Elder came up to my bed side, he said, and asked me if I had faith to be healed. I answered yes. Then said the Elder "In the name of Jesus Christ of Nazareth rise up and walk." And I rose up instantly and walked with the Elder three miles to meeting

that night.   In confirmation of all this he shewed
me the scars on his leg where the breakings out
had been healed.

As the means of investigation were all at
hand, I had not much doubt of the fact, allowing
somewhat for exaggeration, and I merely rela-
ted other wonderful cures that had come to my
knowledge, accounting for them on natural principles. But, said I, if you had faith to be healed,
I suppose you have faith to heal also, and there
are many sick in the neighbourhood.   Yes, he
replied, but they have not faith to be healed, if
they are sick.

In addition to the gifts of healing, the Mormons pretend to prophecy.   As a specimen of
their prophetic gifts ; the Elder declared that
but a short time before, a young Prophetess had
foretold, that on a certain day six persons would
be baptized by immersion, at a distant place ;
and it came to pass, beyond all human calcula-
tion.   The Mormons also pretend to have foretold the natural phenomenon, which took place
on November thirteenth, 1833, and was visible
throughout the United States ; but unfortunately
the prophecy was accomplished before it was
promulgated.

The phenomenon to which I refer, was thus
described in an American Newspaper at the
time.

November 13th, 1833.

Messrs Editors.

A singular phenomenon was exhibited in the

heavens on Wednesday morning, which excited the admiration of all who witnessed its extraordinary appearance, and is well worthy the investigation of scientific enquirers. About four o'clock in the morning, a large meteoric body, resembling a globe of fire, exploded in the Zenith of the heavens, and poured a continuous stream of flaming particles on the sky beneath. The increasing scintillation from this luminous globular body, were showered down like drops of falling rain, illuminating the whole visible horizon, and scattering rich rays of light in each airy path as they fell. After this meteoric shower of fiery rain had for some time descended, a luminous serpentine figure was formed in the sky, which on its explosion, produced a shower of fire equally brilliant and incessant. The inflammatory particles then apparently cohering in one ignited mass, rolled up in a ball to the Zenith; and from this lofty elevation burst, and shot out streams of electric fire from its luminous orb, which continued to fall till the hour of six in the morning, when 'the dawning day put an end to their glory and their flight."

The Mormons profess to have the gift of tongues; and as I had heard a performance of unknown tongues at Mr. Irving's Chapel, in London, I requested the Mormon Elder to favour me with a few sentences, that I might compare them with the "Oh, oh, oh! Ah, ah! Ee-aw, ee-ee, oh! Aw-ah! Eee-aw-oh! Oh, oh, oh, ah,

Ee-aw-aw,-ee-aw!," of our English manifestations ; but in vain.

The Mormons believe, likewise, in the personal reign of Christ, which they predict is to commence in thirty years from this time ; and in the literal restoration of the Jews; but as to the ten tribes of Israel, from whom they say the American Indians are descended, and the " stick of Joseph," they are to be gathered together upon the American continent, and brought in with the fulness of the Gentiles.

If I do not mistake, there are 12,000 of these Mormons. When the sect first sprang up they pitched upon the Western Reserve for their Zion or Promised Land, but finding some difficulty in settlement, they went, for the most part to Missouri ; some of them, however, still remain among the New Settlements, on the shores of Lake Erie.

That many of the Mormon people are perfectly sincere is pretty evident from the sacrifice of property they make. Indeed, they expose themselves without fear to the most contagious diseases, and persist to the death in refusing medical aid. I was acquainted with the case of a young woman in dying circumstances, who could not be persuaded to allow the physician to be called in, although her complaint set all the healing power of the Mormon church at defiance; and, what was worse, her own mother stood at the bed-side, encouraging her obstinacy, and exhorting her to die in the Mormon faith.

But, however credulous and sincere the Mormon *people* may be, unquestionably the *priests* and leaders of Mormonism generally are "wide awake folks," as an Ohioan would express himself, and they find it a profitable game. They have a *regular system* of cheating by the sale of Newspapers &c., in which they promulgate their prophecies, revelations &c., just as fast as expediency will allow. And, as a specimen of their *occasional* tricks, I quote the following from the New York Observer. "We perceive by a letter from Independence, in Missouri, that difficulties have already begun in the Mormon community, at Mount Zion. In that quarter, one of the members having sued a bishop in a court of justice, for fifty dollars, which had been sent by plaintiff to said bishop, from Ohio, to purchase an inheritance for himself and the saints in Zion in these latter days, the jury found for the plaintiff; it appearing that though the bishop had appropriated the money to the purchase of an inheritance, yet he had procured the deed to be drawn in his own name, and to his heirs for ever."

But to conclude, (for I think the reader must be tired of Mormonism) it has come out at last, that the Golden Bible was originally composed for a Novel, and being turned into a Bible by the ingenuity of two or three leading men among the Mormons, was printed and published as the basis of their religion. This developement we trust will speedily extinguish the new lights.

Having said so much about the Mormons we shall pass over the few Shakers, Camelites, and other excrescences of religion, that may be found on the Western Reserve, and proceed to give some account of the regular religious sects.

The Episcopalians are scattered but thinly over the New Settlements, and having no Ministers or Missionaries among them, they generally attend the meetings of other denominations.

The Baptists are more numerous; and many of them are called Free-will Baptists, to distinguish them from others who hold the doctrines of Calvin. Their churches are supplied by Local Preachers, and Missionaries. The description which Mr. W. Ward, the Baptist Missionary, gives of American Baptists in general, will apply equally to those of the Western Reserve, so far as I had an opportunity of judging. "A Baptist church," says Mr. W. in his letter on the State of Society in America, "practising open or *christian* communion I found not; and one or two ministers did not hesitate to avow, that they did not consider pædobaptists as in the pale of the *visible* church !!! Elders, as the scriptural name for ministers, is much used in some parts."

I observe, in passing, that it is common in Ohio to address every man by his proper title, as Elder Phillips, Deacon Brown, &c.

The Methodists have laid out the country into

regular Circuits. Every Society in the Circuits is visited once a fortnight by travelling preachers, and occasionally they are supplied by local preachers and exhorters. Class-meetings, and prayer-meetings are regularly holden on the Sabbath, and during the week; and camp-meetings are not uncommon on the Reserve.

With the Presbyterians I was myself connected, so far as one who had not even put himself under the care of Presbytery, could be connected with that body, being engaged by Presbyterian Churches during the whole time of my residence in Ohio; of the Presbyterians, therefore, I shall give a more particular account.

A great number both of ministers and people who are denominated Presbyterians on the Western Reserve, before their emigration from New England were Congregationalists or Independents; and such they profess to be still, although mingled in the same community with Presbyterians, agreeably to a plan of union between the General Assembly of the Presbyterian Church, and the General Association of Congregationalists in Connecticut. All the independency that I could discern, however, was confined to the discipline of the congregational part of the churches. These mixed churches might hire a Congregationalist Minister, it is true, but unless he connected himself with Presbytery he was not recognized by the Presbyterian Authorities, and the churches to which he preached were pronounced vacant. And if these mixed churches wished to dismiss a minister, who had been regularly installed under the sanction of Presbytery, they must first obtain leave of Presbytery for this purpose. And as to a Congregational or Independent minister, his proceedings with a view to settlement among these mixed churches on the Western Reserve is just the same as among the pure Presbyterian Churches of New York State, or any other State of the Union.

If he be an *ordained* Minister, the following extract of a letter I received from a respected Independent minister who emigrated from this County to America but a few years ago, will direct him in the first step to be taken. " I soon found that this place was vacant, and that if I chose to put myself under the care of Presbytery for twelve months, I could have an opportunity of making a trial here. Accordingly I delivered up my testimonials for examination, and was encouraged to enter the field. My having been ordained saved me from the necessity of applying for license to preach, and opened to me the pulpits of all the ministers. For myself, I am (in this country) neither Independent, nor Dutch, nor Presbyterian, so far, but shall be guided by circumstances at the end of the year. As there is here no *Established Political Church,* the subject of Church Government in a great measure, loses its importance as a question of conscience. * * * I shall be glad to learn how the Northamptonshire brethren go on, and what changes take place among them.

Yours affectionately,

Henry Barber."

If he be *not an ordained minister*, having placed himself under the care of Presbytery for twelve months, he may apply to Presbytery for a license. The Presbytery will then examine him as to his knowledge of the latin language ; and the original languages in which the Scriptures were written. They will examine him also on the arts and sciences; on theology, natural and revealed ; and on ecclesiastical history, the sacraments, church government &c. If his examination proves satisfactory, the Moderator of Presbytery will license him according to the following form.

" In the name of the Lord Jesus Christ, and by that authority which he hath given to the church for its edification, we do license you to preach the gospel, wherever God in his providence may call you : and for this purpose, may the blessing of God rest upon you, and the Spirit of Christ fill your heart.—Amen !"

I would observe here, that in the New Settlements of Ohio, Presbyterians are not so particular in their examinations, and some are licensed who have no acquaintance with the dead languages.

If the candidate who has received a license to preach but *not* a call to be the pastor of a particular congregation, wishes to be ordained to the work of the Gospel ministry, as an evangelist to preach the gospel, administer the ordinances, and organize churches in frontier or destitute settlements; or if he *has* received a call to be the pastor of a particular congregation, he may be ordained by the Presbytery.

The following account of the Dedication of a Church, in connexion with the Ordination of a Minister, at which I was present, may not be uninteresting to the reader.

"FOR THE OHIO OBSERVER.

Messrs. Editors,

At a late meeting of the Presbytery of Cleaveland at Elyria, Feburary 11th, 1834, a new church erected by the first Presbyterian Society of Elyria, was dedicated to the Father, Son, and Holy Ghost, and consecrated for divine worship. The congregation for whom the house was erected, received the same day, in answer to their unanimous call, an *ascension gift*. Mr. James H. Eells, having laboured in this congregation for some months previously, was on that day solemnly set apart, and by prayer, with the laying on the hands of the presbytery, ordained to the Gospel Ministry, and installed Pastor of the congregation in Elyria. The sermon in the morning, at the consecration of the house, was delivered by the Rev. J. Keep, of Cleaveland, and the dedicatory prayer was offered by the Rev. A. H. Betts, of Brownhelim.

In the P. M. the Ordination and Installation services were performed as follows.

Introductory Prayer, offered by Rev. J.
Woodruff—Passages of Scripture, read by Rev.
J. Shailer,—Sermon by Rev. J. Keep,—Ordain-
ing and Installing prayer by Rev. A. H. Betts,—
Right hand of fellowship by the Presbytery pre-
faced by an address from Rev. J. J. Shipherd,—
Charge to the Pastor by Rev. J. Keys,—Charge
to the people by Rev. D. W. Lathrop,—conclud-
ing Prayer by Rev. O. Eastman.

The slips and aisles of the church were
thronged during the day with deeply interested
hearers. The services above named were interspersed with appropriate and excellent music,
both vocal and instrumental, from the Choir in
the gallery, under the direction of the chorister
of the congregation, Mr. B. F. Robinson."

At the Meetings of *Presbytery*, which I attended in these New Settlements, eight or ten
ministers, on an average, were present. They
held their meetings in the Meeting-house. At
every meeting of Presbytery a sermon was delivered; and every particular session was opened
and closed with prayer. If the business brought
before them by delegates from the several
churches within the bounds of Presbytery required, Presbytery sat two or three days in
succession; but if there was little business to
transact, ministers being assembled, would occupy a day or more, according to circumstances,
in preaching for the benefit of that particular
congregation and neighbourhood where they

happened to assemble, visiting the families at intervals of public worship, and endeavouring to leave a blessing behind them.

At the request of a Presbyterian minister, I accompanied him to a meeting of the *Synod* of the Western Reserve and Michigan, which was held at Detroit. We took the Steam-boat, Enterprise, from the Mouth of Huron River, at eight o'clock on Wednesday night, October 9th, 1833, and soon found that there were seventeen ministers on board, besides elders, "chosen men," from all parts of the Reserve, who had embarked at different ports on the Lake Shore, and were all bound to Detroit.

It was a fine star-light night when we put off from Huron, and we sat talking and singing on the upper deck until twelve o'clock. We then went down into the Cabin to steal a little sleep; for as some of us were not Cabin-passengers, we had no regular bed that night, although the next day, seeing that we were likely to be kept out more than one night, we changed our tickets for others which gave us the privileges of the Cabin, and cost us one dollar more, in all two dollars and a half, from Huron to Detroit, a distance of eighty miles.

The little sleep we did steal, however, was soon disturbed; for we had not occupied the cabin-forms along side of the births for more than an hour, before head-winds began to blow violently. The consequence was that we were obliged to put about and take refuge among the

Bass Islands. The Steam-boat, Washington, had been lost on the Lake but a few days before, and our vessel was not in very good trim for a voyage so late in the season; and, altogether, our situation produced considerable anxiety. The sailors, indeed, as usual, attributed the storm to having so many priests on board. And some of the passengers affected to joke, I suppose by way of keeping their courage up; but their jokes were rather forced, and no laugh followed. Others, who had made up beds in the gang-way on the lower deck, were spending their time in prayer. And occasionally, when the tumult was suddenly increased by the overturning of luggage, or of wood piled up for fuel, exclamations of alarm and cries of distress might be heard from the female part of the deck-passengers. The Captain too, went more frequently to the bar. He was a rough brutal fellow. As a proof of which, he would not allow a blessing to be asked at table, saying to the minister who consulted him on the subject, "No, I can eat my victuals without a blessing, and I don't see why you can't. If you want to preach and pray, go ashore, and there you may preach and pray as long as you please." After the danger was over, he acknowledged that if there had not been One above the sailors to take care of us, we should all have gone to the bottom. From three o'clock till daylight, at intervals of sickness, the passengers were anxiously looking out into the surrounding darkness; and, perhaps, none of us felt

the force of the Psalmist's words so much before,
" More than they that watch for the morning."

All day, on Thursday, the Enterprise lay in
Put-in Bay, the very harbour where Perry's
Fleet anchored, after his famous victory, described in the third chapter of this work. In the
morning we went ashore to one of the Bass
Islands, close by the graves of the poor fellows
who had fallen in the battle. There was but
one house in sight, or, perhaps, two joined, and
the appearance of the inmates agreed well with
the wildness of the scenery. I was reminded
of them in my voyage home. In passing the
Cove of Cork, on the Irish Coast, six wild Irish
boys made towards our ship as fast as a rough
sea would allow them, and holding up some fish,
signified that they wanted to sell. Accordingly
a rope was thrown out by which they pulled
their fishing-boat close alongside of us, and a
basket of their fish was drawn aboard. One of
the boys soon followed by the same conveyance,
and as he stood on Quarter Deck, among the
Cabin-passengers, with his bare feet, ragged
clothes, and dripping hair, he presented one of
the most picturesque objects I ever saw in human form. The boy too, seemed to be perfectly
sensible that he had got out of his proper sphere,
for turning his keen eyes round upon the Cabin-
passengers, he said, " It will be many a day
since ye saw the like o' me."

But to return. At eleven o' clock on Thursday night, we left Put-in Bay, and reached De-

troit early on Friday morning. And there we "were received of the church;" two of the members standing ready, as we landed, to take down our names as Ministers and Elders, and to assign us our places of entertainment during the Session of Synod.

Mr. B. and myself were quartered at General Larned's, where we met with a cordial reception, and were entertained the whole week with genuine hospitality. General Larned is the brother of the late Sylvester Larned of New Orleans, of whose life and character he gave us some interesting particulars. It appears that from his youth, Sylvester Larned was possessed of extraordinary powers, both of body and mind, aud after his conversion to God, the decision of character and daring zeal which he manifested, were not less remarkable. As soon as he completed his studies for the ministry he determined to visit New Orleans, "Because," said he, "it is the citadel of infidelity." When he arrived there was not a Protestant Church in the whole city; the Sabbath was scarcely to be distinguished from any other day in the week; and profligacy of manners prevailed to a fearful extent. Mr. Larned commenced his attack upon this "citadel," by preaching in a hired room to all who would come and hear him; but in a short time so rapidly did his congregation increase, that they built a splendid Church and offered him a salary of four thousand dollars per annum. His talents commanded the attention of all classes; and among the rest of his admir-

ers was a maniac, who availed himself of every
lucid interval to cultivate his acquaintance, and
would be controlled by him alone. One day
this maniac visited Mr. Larned, and proposed
that they should take a walk out into the sub-
urbs of the city. Accordingly they walked
arm in arm, until they came to a retired spot;
when the maniac drawing a dagger from his
bosom, where he had kept his right hand during
their walk, and elevating his arm at the same
time, said to Mr. Larned "You're a dead man."
Mr. Larned, in an instant, bared his breast to
the madman, and exclaimed with his tremendous
voice "In the name of the Living God I defy
you!" The maniac dropping the dagger at his
feet melted into tears, and from that moment
has had the perfect possession of his reason.

Detroit is a large thriving town, and very
much frequented by Indians. The appearance
of a bony Indian, six feet high at least, walking
along empty handed, while his poor feeble
squaw (wife) at his side, seemed ready to sink
at every step under a heavy burden, confirmed
the general opinion, that the man of America is
an unkind husband. But he disdains the
charge. He says, "The men among us suffer
all the hardships of war; and in peace, we sometimes hunt from day to day without success,
hungry and faint, while our women are comfortable at the lodge. The women own all the
children; the lodge and the wigwam are theirs,
and all the household furniture. The men own

the guns, the traps, the powder and lead, the horses and canoes. The women and children own the fishing lines and hooks, the axes and the hoes. We kill the bear, the deer, and the otter, the mink, and the muskrat. The women and children sometimes catch the fish, kill the birds, and raise the corn. We teach the boys hunting. The women teach the girls to cook, to make mats of rushes and various kinds of bark, to dress skins, and make them into mocasins, ornamented with porcupine quills."

The Meeting of Synod was held in the Presbyterian Church, and about forty ministers were present. As at Meetings of Presbytery, and General Assembly, an introductory sermon was delivered, and each particular session was opened and closed with prayer. A moderator and clerk were then chosen after the usual manner. Statistical Reports were read, and Narratives of Religion. Bible Society, Missionary Society, Education Society, and other business was attended to from day to day. On the Sabbath the Ordinance of the Lord's Supper was publicly administered. And the whole was conducted with perfect order and good feeling.

With respect to the *Sabbath* in these New Settlements, many Christians in Ohio, as well as New England, commence its exercises on the Saturday evening, and terminate them on Sabbath evening at *sundown ;* as some parents tell their children, when they can count ten stars.

There are Sabbath scenes in some of the
thinly settled districts of Ohio, that would present a novel appearance to an Englishman.
The place of worship, situated on the side of a
road, newly cut through the midst of the woods,
is none other than a log-house of the rudest description ; with a stick chimney, and a door that
opens to the pulling of a string that hangs down
without. The bare ground serves for a hearth
within, which is furnished with two or three
large stones, destined in winter, to sustain the
huge pile of a wood fire. When the sun's elevation indicates the time of meeting, the inhabitants of the township may be seen issuing from
the woods in every direction, some on foot, and
some on horseback ; but most of them in ox-
waggons, containing eight or ten individuals,
which were partly gathered on the way, thus
going from strength to strength, from company
to company. During service, the horses are
hitched to the trees about the Meeting-house,
and in wet weather, the saddles are brought inside ; the yoked oxen stand along the zigzag
fences, feasting upon hay or the stalks of Indian
corn. With regard to the accommodations for
worship inside, the minister is provided with an
old chair and table; the people are seated on
forms; or, if the house happens to be crowded,
some mount the desks which are fixed round the
room for the use of the school. The congregation, too, have a singular appearance, especially
in summer, since all the men leave their coats

at home, and some of the women their bonnets
also, if they have any, for they come to Meeting
with nothing but a coloured handkerchief tied
about the head. Nevertheless, what clothes
they do wear are clean; the white shirt sleeves
of the men give a lively air to the scene at any
rate; and were it not for the tobacco *chawing*
and spitting, every thing might be said to be
done decently and in order.

The reader will take notice that this is a
Sabbath-scene of the lowest order, even among
the New Settlements, which contain many good
Meeting-houses and respectable congregations;
and it is as different from the Sabbath-scenes in
the villages of Ohio as of England, the churches
in these villages being spacious and elegant, all
steepled, as if to assert the equality of all denominations, and every one furnished with a bell.

It is not common among the religious people
in America to cook dinners on the Sabbath-day.
In the New Settlements the Meeting-house is
situated centrally to the congregation, and so far
from most of them, as not to admit of their returning home at noon; consequently, the greater
part remain all day, and take what refreshment
they bring with them, between the services.

About half an hour after the morning service
terminates, the exercises of the Sabbath-school,
and of the Bible-class commence. In connexion
with the Sabbath-school, there is always a
library of interesting and instructive books,
chiefly illustrative of Scripture. These books

the scholars read during the week, and exchange
on the Sabbath-day ; and the library constitutes
not only a very useful branch of Sabbath-school
privileges, but to the children, perhaps, the most
attractive. The children, however, do not attend Sabbath-schools, for the purpose of learning
to read, as in England, but to apply the talent of
reading, which they acquire at week-day
schools, to subjects consonant with the Sabbath.
When properly qualified for its exercises, the
Sabbath-school children are admitted to the
Bible-class : not that the Bible-class is confined
to young people, for it includes the deacons and
members of the church generally, with any
others, who may desire to avail themselves of
its advantages, both male and female. The minister opens the Bible-class with prayer, and
then proceeds to ask those questions upon the
appointed lesson which are best adapted to the
capacities of the various members of the class ;
giving the critical import of the text, explaining
the difficulties suggested, and making practical
observations. On some occasions, the exercises
of the Bible-class are very interesting, as general preparation is made during the week for a
creditable examination ; and it is not uncommon
for the farmers to possess Scott's Commentary
at home, or some other help to a right understanding of the Scriptures.

The Bible-class exercise continues about an
hour, and is followed, almost immediately, by
the regular service of the afternoon ; after

which, the congregation disperse to their several homes; and during the evening, little groups of them meet in different parts of the township, for conference or prayer-meetings. These meetings are held in School-houses or private houses; during the summer, when the sun is *an hour high*, or at *early candlelight;* and even in winter, when the roads are bad, and the nights dark, some will travel a mile or two for the purpose of attending a prayer-meeting, lighting themselves through the woods by torches, composed of long strips of hickory bark, which they hold in their hands, and brighten occasionally, as they go, by knocking off the burnt ends of them against the trees.

The minister conducts the meetings, when he is present; but it is common for the deacons, or members of the church to deliver addresses, as well as to lead in prayer; and being well versed in Scripture, and accustomed to public speaking, they do it, in many instances, with great propriety. Having addressed the meeting himself, perhaps, the minister concludes by saying—"If any brother has remarks to make, we shall be glad to hear them." And when he has named any person to lead in prayer, he adds, "If any brother should feel disposed to continue the devotions before we rise from our knees, he will have an opportunity." By this general permission, at conference, or prayer-meetings, the best talents are called into exercise, and the best feelings are diffused; and the interest of the meeting is not thrown at the mercy of one or two giftless, graceless individuals. This course is commonly pursued by the Presbyterians on the Reserve, nor did I ever know it abused.

Religion in these New Settlements, is supported on the voluntary principle, as throughout the United States. I had thought, indeed, that Massachusetts still retained the right of taxing her inhabitants for the support of religion; but according to Mr. Colton, this "last relic of a State Establishment in America," is abolished. The salaries of ministers in the villages of Ohio average about four hundred dollars, and in the New Settlements two hundred dollars; in the former, a single gentleman may obtain board and lodging, with good accommodations, for two dollars per week; and in the latter, for twelve shillings of American money.

In many of the New Settlements, little can be spared for the support of religion, at present, by those who are inclined to be liberal, and others want the inclination. Were they idolators, I apprehend but few of them could afford a graven image, spread over with gold and adorned with silver chains; and some of those few, I guess, preferring to keep their silver in the shape of hard dollars, if they must have a god, would hasten to the woods, and choose "a tree that will not rot."

In such cases as these, the Presbyterian minister receives fifty or a hundred dollars per an-

num from the Home Missionary Society, and
the people make up the remainder. Generally
speaking, too, the ministers are pluralists, having two or more churches under their care. These
churches or congregations *hire* the minister, as
they express it, half the time, or a third of the
time. And, sometimes, Settlements, that have
no professing Christians among them, will hire
a minister to preach to them one Sabbath in a
month, just to save appearances. I once
preached to such a Settlement, and the following extract from a letter, written at the time,
will give you some idea of the place and the
people.

" The mouth of River—— is five miles from
hence ; and the road which lies along the banks
of the river, is pleasant enough in summer, but
in winter, dirty and dreary. The opposite side of
the road from the river is wood, and, occasionally, one comes to an opening in which the ruins
of a log-house, broken down zigzag fences, and
a few garden herbs, running wild, show where
some poor fellow had begun to struggle for a
living, but, not being able to get along, moved
out. The first four miles of the road is uninhabited ; not because the soil is barren, but
partly because it has got a bad name for fever
and ague, and partly because the land is dear.
In passing along towards the Lake, R.'s tavern
appears in the distance, together with two or
three smart frame stores, and about a dozen
dwelling houses, situated very pleasantly on the

banks of the Lake, beyond the river. Within
a quarter of a mile from the place of crossing
is a barn, where I put up my horse until I returned from meeting. From this barn, I walked
to the bank of the river on the Lake shore, sinking at every step in the shining sands, thrown
up by the waves: for here the shore is almost
on a level with the Lake, but generally, the bank
is broken and precipitate, twelve or fifteen feet
above the surface of the water; and the soil,
being soft, the inroads which the Lake makes
upon its banks is so rapid, that in some places,
it has almost reached the fences, which part off
the road on the opposite side from the fields.
The trees, also, which formerly hid the Lake
from the road, being gradually undermined by
the water, fall as the bank gives way and are
soon buried beneath the drifted sands. Before
I cross the river, I will give you some account
of the inhabitants on the other side. The father
of the Settlement was Squire R., who was one
of the first settlers on this part of the Reserve.
Two anecdotes of the old Squire, who is now
dead and gone, will give some idea of his character. It was customary with him, when he
killed a pig, to ask a blessing upon it, and that
blessing served till the whole pig was eaten. It
is said, also, that a minister took up his lodging
at the Squire's tavern one night, and when he
asked the Squire in the morning what he had to
pay, the Squire told him that he should not
take any thing. " Why," said the minister,

"although I am a minister, I have had no religious conversation with you; we have had no family prayer—" "That's the very reason," interrupted the Squire, "why I don't charge you any thing." The influence which the first settlers have upon the future character of their townships is strikingly exhibited at the Mouth of —— River. Squire R. gradually gathered round him seventeen or eighteen families, all of the same description with himself, who regard religion as a necessary evil, the ministry as a trade, and, as one of them said, "pay the priest as they pay the fiddler." Frequently, on the Sabbath-morning, did I see the people shooting, or skaiting, or working, as I rode along towards the Settlement. But now we may cross the river, whicn I did in summer by a canoe, and in winter on the ice. About a quarter of a mile from the river, at the extremity of this little cluster of white frame buildings stands the School-house, itself a pretty frame building, about the size of your vestry. It is situated within a dozen yards of the Lake; so that in rough weather we could scarcely hear each other speak at the School-house door, on account of the roaring of the waves. The natural scenery was foreign, but the character of the congregation much more so. Instead of the simple hearted, affectionate congregations that meet one in English villages, there were a few hardened infidels, as blind to spiritual things as the dark woods, and as deaf to the invitations of the

gospel as the boisterous seas around them. As
to singing at our meetings, frequently there was
none. And in prayer, a presbyterian minister
who used to preach at the same place, observed,
" I could never say *our* Father."

The Emigrant will find many temptations
to settle in such a township as that I have described above, but if he should yield to such a
temptation, it will be ridiculous for him to complain, as some have done under similar circumstances, of a deficiency in religious privileges.
There is abundance of good land on the Reserve
and cheap, which may be obtained, within convenient distance of a regular ministry ; and of
all Emigrants, I have observed, that those are
best satisfied with their change, who unite
themselves with christian churches, and enter
most fully into the spirit of the various efforts
made by Americans for the promotion of religion
and morality.

CHAPTER VII.

> " Think not that you are no enthusiast, then :
> All men are such, as sure as they are men.
> The thing itself is not at all to blame :
> 'Tis in each state of human life the same.
> That which concerns us, therefore, is to see
> What species of enthusiasts we be.
> Blame not enthusiasm if rightly bent,
> Or blame of saints the holiest intent :
> When true religion kindles up the fire,
> Who can condemn the vigorous desire ?"

" It is remarkable," says Mr. Colton, " that revivals of religion under their American character, commenced in New England, and were, till quite recently principally confined to that region. And their extension westward and southward," he believes, " has generally been found in the track of New England Emigrants."

In accordance with this last remark, I may observe that the revival which I design to narrate in this chapter, took place among New Englanders principally; and what is more, I have reason to believe, it originated in the prayers and tears of an excellent individual, who traces his descent to one of those very Pilgrim Fathers that landed on the rock at Plymouth in 1662.

As an apology for writing more upon a subject which has occupied so much abler pens of late, I observe in the first place, that this work may fall into the hands of many who never have seen, and perhaps never will see, the larger and more important publications of Colton, Sprague, and others. And, in the second place, as a revival of vegetation in Spring, presents a variety of aspect at different times and places, and under different circumstances, so it is with a revival of religion. I trust, therefore, that the following narrative will be neither uninteresting nor unprofitable.

The phrase, Revival of Religion, then, I observe, is used in America to express the renewed spiritual prosperity of any church ; and it includes, also, the conversion of sinners. As it relates to any church, a revival of religion, of course, implies a previous decline.

By a decline of religion, I do not mean the neglect of its outward form. He that walketh in the midst of the seven golden candlesticks did not charge the Churches of Asia with neglecting the external forms of Christianity, yet he censures their declension. Nay, he admits many things to their credit, which perhaps are not commonly found in the Churches of the present day. Read, for example, what is said of the Church of Ephesus, " And hast borne, and hast patience, and for my name's sake hast laboured and hast not fainted. Nevertheless saith He that holdeth the seven stars in his right hand

" I have somewhat against thee, because thou hast left thy first love," In this very thing consisted the declension of religion at Vermillion, as I shall presently show.

Vermillion is the name of a township, about five miles square, bounded on the east by Vermillion river, and by Lake Erie on the north. Its inhabitants are five hundred in number, more or less; all holding land, with the exception of about fifteen or twenty families that are employed at the furnace.

The Presbyterian church at Vermillion, consists of seventy members; and when I entered upon my duties among them, family worship was maintained; one evening in the week, at least, they held a conference or prayer-meeting, both at the Ridge, and at the Lake shore; and on the Sabbath-day, (considering that the meeting-house was situated in the midst of the woods, two or three miles from the greater part of the congregation; considering, too, that the weather was severe, for it was winter, and the roads bad) there was as good an attendance as could reasonably be expected. Besides all this, subscriptions were regularly, and in some instances, liberally paid to the Bible, Missionary, and Education Societies, by professing Christians at Vermillion; yet I found them lamenting their spiritual declension. They had left their first love.

Of course, a decline of religion is greater or less in different churches, and in different individuals of the same church before a revival takes place. From the public and private confessions made by the church of Vermillion, previous to their revival, it appeared that with some of them the tide of spiritual feeling had sunk to a very low ebb indeed. About a fortnight before the Protracted Meeting, a day of fasting and prayer was observed on account of this religious declension. During the exercises of the day, considerable feeling was manifested by the deacons and members of the church in general, and many tears were shed; yet some still prayed and spoke as if that which remained of grace within them was " ready to die."

At the close of the services on that fast-day, it was proposed that a Protracted Meeting should be appointed for the earliest period that the assistance of neighbouring ministers could be obtained. There was only one man who objected to it, and he was the principal supporter of the gospel in the place. " Brethren," said he, " I know it will avail nothing to have a protracted meeting, unless the members of the church feel right. Now," he continued, " I, for one, do not feel right: I scarcely feel at all. My prayers and religious services in general, for these last three months, have been little else than formality. And, indeed, since I joined the church fourteen years ago, I guess I never felt so little of the power of religion. I doubt, at times, whether I have not been deceiving myself with false hopes. I think I do rejoice to

P

hear of revivals in other places; but then, again, I suspect this rejoicing to be only because my own particular denomination of Christians is increased."

Several others complained of similar insensibility; and especially during the few weeks preceding the revival. It was darkest just before the dawn.

Such being a decline of religion, observe, further, the *means* which God employs in America for reviving his work.

Professing Christians in England regard a Revival of Religion as a desirable thing; but, as soon as I became acquainted with the state of feeling prevalent in the infant churches of Ohio, I observed, that if they were not actually enjoying a revival, they were on the look out. They waited "for the Lord, more than they that watch for the morning." Many of them had been converted at revivals in the eastern country, and most of them had breathed the hallowed atmosphere. Their churches were gradually augménting by the accession of individuals; but they had enjoyed special outpourings of the Holy Spirit—they had seen, in some instances, multitudes added to the Church the same day; and they talked, and preached, and prayed, as if a gradual work not only did not, but ought not to satisfy them.

This state of feeling is kept alive in the New Settlements of Ohio, by newspapers, revival magazines, &c., which circulate reports of every revival that takes place, not only in America, but throughout the world.

Among private Christians, revivals constitute a prominent topic of conversation.

Ministers, also, bring it forward from the pulpit, at Conference Meetings, and in their pastoral visits.

But the most successful efforts for reviving the Churches of the Western Reserve, that have come to my knowledge, were made under the conduct of Evangelists, ministers of the Congregational or Presbyterian denomination, who travel about the country with this object in view; and, for support, are hired by vacant Churches a few weeks at a time, or receive voluntary contributions, in return for assistance rendered to settled pastors.

The most powerful means, however, sometimes fail. One of these Evangelists whose labours had been greatly blessed in other places, visited the village of E. The Church was vacant, and he was hired for three months. It was an important station, and he left nothing untried that might rouse the church to duty. Meetings were better attended; more sermons were preached, more prayers were offered, and more hymns were sung, but the state of feeling remained much the same. We looked for an effectual moving of the water, but scarcely any thing more was to be seen than a certain restlessness natural to the element.

In other cases, revivals occur when no extraordinary means are used, but when every thing seems to be against them. A solitary sinner, perhaps, is converted, and goes about among his neighbours to tell

" What a dear Saviour he has found."

Or, two or three members of the church meet together in a log-house and pray for a revival; and look, and pray, and look again, until the little cloud ariseth out of the sea, like a man's hand, and there is a great rain. Or, some simple sentiment falling from the preacher's lips drops like a spark among combustible matter, and fires the whole church : as if God were determined to give a practical illustration of the text, "It is not by might, nor by power, but by my spirit saith the Lord."

With respect to the external means used at Vermillion before the Revival, the subject was urged upon the attention of the church in public and private, for several weeks in succession; additional prayer and conference-meetings were held, and one whole day was given to fasting and prayer. At first, the excitement was confined to one or two individuals, but by such means as these it gradually spread and increased, until, with very few exceptions, the whole church was revived.

Observe, finally, the nature of a Revival, as it respects the church, or how it manifests itself.

It is manifested by deep repentance.

The first thing an Evangelist does when he visits any church, with a view to its revival, is to lay before that church the guilt of its declension. If the church does not repent after the subject has been repeatedly and earnestly pressed upon their attention, he leaves them and goes on to the next; well assured that if Christians cannot see, or will not feel, the guilt of their falling, they will never exert themselves to recover the heights from whence they have fallen. But if there be any indications of penitence in the Church—if their ingratitude to the Saviour, and the deadly influence which their indifference has exerted upon sinners, appear to humble them, he is encouraged to persevere, and a revival follows.

The humiliation and brokenness of heart, which appeared in the Church at Vermillion, were remarkable. I had seen the sinner humbled to the dust before God, when he was first brought to repentance; and I had seen the backslider, who had brought a reproach upon the cause of Christ by immorality, returning with weeping and supplication; but to see a Church like that of Vermillion, as described in the first part of this chapter, humbling themselves to tears, was a new thing. Many of them could scarcely ever allude to their past lukewarmness without weeping; and their prayers and addresses were often interrupted by bursts of sorrow. Before sinners, they confessed their inconsistent conduct in not labouring more diligently for the glory of God and the salvation of souls, and thereby wiped off the reproach from religion, and took it upon themselves.

A Revival is characterized also by a spirit of ardent prayer for the conversion of sinners.

Before the signal outpouring of the Spirit's influences on the day of Pentecost, the disciples continued with one accord in prayer and supplication, and so it is before every genuine revival. In the Report of a revival which took place in Ohio, some months before I left, it was stated that the members of the Church continued praying all night even until break of day. And at Vermillion in several instances they prayed till midnight in private houses after the public services of the day. They did not go to prayer-meetings to get a spirit of prayer, but to pour out the fulness of their hearts before the Lord, to disburthen their oppressed spirits. Hence I observed that much of the usual introduction to prayer was dispensed with, and the objects of prayer were hurried as it were to the mercy seat, and presented with an importunity truly affecting. They travailed in birth for souls, and being in an agony, prayed. When they looked into the faces of their impenitent friends and relatives, they had such a realizing sense of the value of their souls, and of their imminent danger of damnation, that they had enough to do to restrain their feelings; and in spite of every effort, the deep anxiety of their souls would occasionally burst into tears and sobbing. One individual, and that was none other than the person who scarcely felt at all on the fast-day, after praying with others till midnight for the conversion of his fellow sinners, was so much concerned for the salvation of an infidel neighbour, that, from the prayer-meeting he proceeded to the house of that neighbour, and earnestly entreated him to attend the protracted meeting, and delay no longer the great concerns of his soul.

This is a little "wild fire," some will say; and I take the opportunity of observing, that it is not my design in this chapter to tell what a Protracted Meeting *ought to be*, but what it *was;* not how I felt myself, but how others felt. Every man has a standard of his own by which he tries religious excitement; and, unquestionably, if the state of feeling I have described above be not condemned by many professing Christians, the way in which that feeling manifested itself at Vermillion will form a subject for ridicule. The opinion which may be passed however upon the feeling, or the manifestation of feeling with regard to the "Great things" of God's Law is worthy of respect, or contemptible, just in proportion as it hath, or hath not, the sanction of that Law. For my own part, I must confess that what I saw at Vermillion reminded me very forcibly of many passages of Scripture; e. g. "Rivers of waters run down mine eyes, because they keep not thy law." "And when he was come near, he beheld the city, and wept

over it, &c." " And others save with fear pulling them out of the fire." And I have sometimes thought, too, that however we may feel
disposed to blame the individual who went to
his neighbour at midnight, and besought him to
flee from the wrath to come, (which was a solitary case) that if St. Paul had passed along at the
time, he might possibly have commended his zeal;
for St. Paul was not ashamed of telling Christians, " By the space of three years, I ceased not
to warn every one night and day with tears."
And certainly the apparent self-annihilation
among God's people, and their tender yearning
over impenitent parents and children, brethren
and sisters, &c. at Vermillion, formed the best
illustration I have seen of those remarkable
words, " I say the truth in Christ, I lie not, my
conscience also bearing me witness in the Holy
Ghost, that I have great heaviness and continual
sorrow in my heart. For I could wish that myself were accursed from Christ for my brethren,
my kinsmen according to the flesh."

Again, a Revival of religion manifests itself
in union of feeling, and co-operation of effort,
for the salvation of sinners.

Love to the brethren is revived on such occasions. It is very common for Christians in
Ohio to address each other by the name of brother; and brotherly love is very much promoted
by their Conference Meetings, when Christians
are in the habit of expressing their feelings to
each other, and of sympathizing with each other,

with respect to the state of their minds &c. But this union among Christians is peculiarly striking at Revivals. If any difference has existed among Christians of the same church, it is no uncommon thing for them to come forward before the congregation, each of them confessing himself most to blame, and taking the other's hand in token of reconciliation. Members of other Presbyterian Churches, some of them twelve or fifteen miles off, attended the Protracted Meeting at Vermillion, and were entertained by their christian brethren with the utmost cordiality; indeed, a kind of open house was kept by Christians at Vermillion, during the whole time of the Meeting.

Besides this, the Methodists co-operated with the Presbyterians in promoting the conversion of sinners. Squire S., a Justice of the Peace at Vermillion, and a leading man among the Methodists, attended the prayer-meetings on the fast-day mentioned above; and being requested to address the congregation, he spoke to the following effect. "Brethren," said he, "I bless God for bringing me here to-day. Some of us well recollect the meetings we held some two or three years ago in the old School-house on the Ridge. They were refreshing seasons, brethren! How sweet their memory still! But, alas! religion has declined very much among us of late; for one, at least, I may say, it is not with me as in months that are past. I rejoice, however, to see the slightest indication of a revival. I care not, brethren, whether a revival begins with the Presbyterians, or Baptists, or Methodists; I want to see all revived. And, although I have not consulted the members of the Methodist Society, yet I know I may offer you their hearty co-operation in any efforts you may make for the conversion of sinners." Accordingly, Methodists were appointed to accompany Presbyterians in visiting every family of Vermillion, previously to the Protracted Meeting. And, as the township was laid out into districts, and two visitors were appointed for every district, it sometimes happened that one Methodist and one Presbyterian went through a district in company, calling at every house, exhorting the people and praying with them, and entreating them to attend the Meeting. In fact, the union of feeling among Christians at Vermillion, reminded us of the effect produced by the outpouring of the Spirit on the day of Pentecost. " And all that believed were together, and had all things common—continuing daily with one accord in the temple, and breaking bread from house to house, did eat their meat with gladness and singleness of heart, praising God, and having favour with all the people. And the Lord added to the Church daily such as should be saved."

I do not mean to say that sectarianism never appears at such meetings. On the contrary, this accursed spirit sometimes nips the bud of promise, when every thing seems to bid fair for a revival; and, at other times, it checks a revival after successful progress has been made. A genuine revival of religion is absolutely incompatible with a sectarian spirit; and all those who are actuated by such a spirit can do no more than convert young Christians to their peculiar views respecting the non-essentials of Christianity, after they have been converted to God. And, for this purpose, they watch a revival, as so many kites or vultures hovering over a battle field.

It is a common mistake with reference to the Revivals in America, that it is all done at Protracted Meetings—that whatever effect may be produced, commences and terminates within a few days. So far from this, Protracted Meetings are appointed in consequence of a revival in the church, and solely for the conversion of sinners. A Protracted Meeting is an extra effort, made by any church in behalf of sinners, to bring them under the sound of the gospel in circumstances calculated to prepare them for its cordial reception.

The common name of these Meetings in Ohio, is "Four-day Meetings," because, under ordinary circumstances, they are held four days. But, if the interest excited will support it—if the success demands it, they are protracted to weeks and even months.

The Meeting at Vermillion was held eight days in succession. Not a stroke of work was done. Every day was a Sabbath. The congregation assembled about nine o'clock in the morning, some on foot, some on horseback, and others in waggons. The Meeting opened with prayer. After the prayer-meeting there was a sermon and regular service which continued till noon, when there was a few minutes intermission. During this intermission, the congregation partook of whatever eatables they had brought with them, and for drink were supplied from the brook that flows by. The afternoon services were as the morning; and about four o'clock the people repaired to their homes, in the several parts of the township, and attended evening meetings.

The sermons at these Meetings were preached chiefly by two neighbouring Presbyterian Ministers who had been long accustomed to conduct Protracted Meetings in different parts of America. Each of them preached two regular discourses, four or five days in succession, and otherwise abounded in private labours. Contrary to what I had observed at other Protracted Meetings, if the preachers had notes they made little or no use of them. Their style of preaching was pointed, often pathetic, and sometimes very powerful.

With regard to the order of their discourses &c., the first day of the Meeting was more private, being spent in addressing the church and in prayer. Among the directions suggested, relative to the Meeting, were such as these. "Don't depend upon the Ministers, but look to

God for success. Leave the world at home. Talk little during intermissions; and what you do say, let it be confined to the great work before us. Don't criticize the sermons, nor make comparisons. If you observe any persons affected by the discourses, don't tell it, lest it, come to their ears and disgust them, &c."

The tendency of the first discourses was to excite the Church to untiring exertion, and earnest prayer. Alarming sermons were then preached to sinners from such texts as these " The wages of sin is death: or pathetic subjects were presented from, " Being grieved for the hardness of their hearts, &c." And when sinners began to be awakened, the discourses were calculated to bring them to decision, or to direct them, &c.

As to the doctrine preached at this Meeting, I observe that the preachers did not tell the sinner to repent, believing in their hearts the while, that the sinner could not repent; and having no other reason to assign for their exhortation than this, " We are commanded to say, Repent!" Nor did the preachers tell the sinner to use the means and God would bring him to repentance; for they had the sinner under the means already. Nor did the preachers explain the way in which a sinner may turn to God, according to the theory of " Voluntary thought" and " Voluntary attention." They believed one of their own Reviewers on this theory of moral agency. " First, it removes no difficulty. The

Q

fact to be accounted for, is an act of choice,—
a man's taking God for his portion. Mr. Hinton's
solution is '*voluntary* attention,' i. e. choice to
consider a subject. But one act of choice plainly
needs as much to be accounted for as another;
and therefore we must resort again to his solution, to account for this preceding choice. Here
then is a *choice* to consider, whether we shall
choose to reflect, on the subject of *choosing* to
obey God! And thus we may go back without
end; we are brought at once to the old absurdity
of an infinite series." Nor did the preachers tell
the sinner that he could repent *if* he would, but
he had no power to will. Their sentiments on
this subject, I know from private conversation,
coincided with the following statement of one
of their favourite preachers. "Nothing can be
more delusive than the idea of power or ability
resulting from the mere possession of the *facul-
ties* of understanding, will, and conscience, while
an *if* is introduced, an absolute negation inter-
posed, as to something lying back of these in
the constitution of the mind, without which the
will can in the *nature of things* act only one way.
It is just like saying of a steam-boat at the
wharf, having paddles and an engine;—that
boat has 'full power' to move this moment, *if
the fire were only kindled*. But has it power to
kindle the fire for itself? By no means. Then
of what value or importance is the 'full power,'
or 'natural ability' you speak of? If it were a
living conscious agent, would it be *bound* to

kindle up that fire, when its power, as you affirm, extends not to the furnace, but only to the engine and the wheels. But God *does* require sinners to kindle up the fire in their own hearts. The whole difficulty in the case is settled aversion. Though this aversion be so strong that no human being, left to himself, will ever subdue it, it is nothing but aversion still. Though bearing in a *figurative sense*, the name of inability, to express its strength and permanence, it has never, in true New England usage, implied any *if*, any want of power to *be* at once well disposed—to do the very thing commanded by God, 'make you a new heart.'" These, I say, were the private sentiments of the preachers, so far as I could ascertain. In their public preaching, they took God's part decidedly against the sinner. They told him he had destroyed *himself*, and that it would be his own fault if he were not saved. They took it for granted that the sinner could repent, and that he knew it. And as if they had never heard of the controversy respecting natural and moral inability, they came forward with Apostolic boldness, commanding and entreating him to repent and turn to God.

The preaching of ministers at this Meeting was seconded by the prayers of the people. Sometimes the Meeting-house was so full that professing Christians retired to the School-house to pray. And on one occasion, the School-house was crowded with females who occupied it for a Prayer-meeting; whilst the men to the number of about two hundred, went out into the woods, and seated themselves on the logs, or the bare ground, lifting up their voices in prayer and thanksgiving to Him, who is not confined to temples made with hands. But the prayers of the Church were not limited by public services. In those parts of the township where they could not obtain preaching in the evenings, prayer-meetings were held. And, indeed, if but two or three happened to meet in a private house, during the intervals of public worship, they would have a *season of prayer*.

With the preaching and prayers, the hymns and style of singing were in perfect unison, being of a solemn and affecting kind, calculated to alarm the careless sinner, and to encourage the penitent.

But we must proceed to the next general division of the subject which relates to *the conversion of sinners*.

In many cases, when the Church is prepared in an extraordinary degree to receive a blessing, the effect of such means as I have described is almost immediate. But at Vermillion, the preaching continued three days before there was any visible awakening among sinners. On the fourth day of the Meeting, the word preached began to lay hold on the feelings of sinners and to take effect. At the close of the service those who felt anxious about their salvation, and wished to enjoy an interest in the prayers and counsels of God's people, were requested to come

forward and occupy a seat which was vacated
for them, called the *Anxious Seat*. On the first
invitation, about twelve came forward; and the
number gradually increased during the following
days, until forty or fifty were seen upon the
anxious seat.

Some of them had been long impressed with
the importance of religion, and by that meeting
were brought to a decision. Among these, I
might mention the eldest brother of Euphemia
S. whose funeral is described in the fourth chapter of this work. From the death of his sister this
youth evinced deep and constant anxiety respecting his state as a sinner before God; at the
Protracted Meeting, he obtained the hope of
pardon, and experienced that peace which pass-
eth all understanding. Euphemia's father, also,
who had conducted himself as a consistent Christian for many years, and had often been solicited
to unite himself with God's professing people, at
this meeting came to the determination to give
himself to the Church. The father and son both
intended to propose themselves for Church-
membership the first opportunity, and I have no
doubt long e'er this, have celebrated the dying
love of Christ together. And thus, as the pious
mother of Euphemia said, when I expressed my
surprise at her attending the Protracted Meeting
so constantly with her infant child, "I do not
regret it, Sir, I have received a double blessing."

Others attended the Meeting solely on account of the entreaties of their Christian friends, who seemed as anxious to bring them as if it was their only chance of salvation. Nor were the exertions made to bring such persons under the sound of the gospel, nor were the prayers offered for a blessing, in vain. Some, it is true, passed through the revival unaffected; but others were humbled to the dust. One sinner, especially, who hardened his neck, and stoutly resisted all the influences bearing upon his conscience and his heart, for six days in succession, at last yielded the contest, and came like a little child, weeping to the Anxious Seat. It was sublime to see a man who had scoffed at religion, and who had trifled with every thing sacred, but a few days before, come out from the midst of his infidel companions, and, before their very eyes, take his seat with penitents. I had seen the floods of Niagara, and had heard its thunders, but it struck me as a more wondrous exhibition of Divine power, thus to bend the stubborn will and bow the haughty spirit of Vermillion sinners.

"Now," said Mr. J. to these mourning souls, "you may think that we pity you as unfortunate, but no, we dare not take your part. We can regard you in no other light than that of rebels against God. You appear to be deeply affected with your condition as sinners, and so indeed you ought to be; but after all you may be far from possessing true religion—from being the subjects of renewing grace—from submitting to God. Now there is no other way of salvation than by absolute unconditional submission to God. You must feel and acknowledge that God is right, and that you are wrong. You must give up the controversy. God will accept you on no other terms. You know the conditions; you have your choice. If you will risk damnation rather than bow, we cannot help it; all that we can do is to weep over you."

After such exhortations as these, a minister, or one of the members of the Church would pray *aloud* in their behalf; or, as on one occasion, the whole Church and congregation interceded for these anxious sinners in *silent prayer*. The meeting throughout was characterized by solemnity; there was a sacred awe upon the minds of the people during the week, which rebuked every thing like lightness of conversation, even at home; the outspread wings of the Heavenly Dove appeared to overshadow their dwellings: but those few minutes of *silent prayer* for distressed souls were solemn as eternity; it was the crisis of immortal destinies; and not a breath was heard, save the indications of distress from the anxious seat, which could not be repressed.

But the scene out of doors was not less interesting, on some occasions, than within. In one part of the woods, you might see Christians pleading with their wicked neighbours; and in another, dejected and disconsolate sinners mourning apart. There were two brothers at this meeting that excited much sympathy. The elder of them had been converted at a similar meeting, and at the same place, three years before; but the younger, according to his own confession afterwards, was "The greatest sinner in Huron County." In answer to the prayers of the Christian, however, and as the reward of his anxious exertions, he had the unspeakable satisfaction of seeing his poor wandering brother brought home to God. He was amongst the earliest and most decided trophies of redeeming grace and dying love, at the meeting; and the heart was made of adamant that did not melt to see the two brothers, walking hand in hand from the Meeting-house, tears of gratitude and joy streaming down their faces as they went. At the evening meeting, the same day, I requested the young convert to express his feelings; he complied with my request, and told a tale that dissolved the whole congregation to tears.

But this was not the only one who rejoiced in answer to prayer. On one occasion those who *indulged a hope*, were requested to rise, and the number was upwards of forty; many others were deeply impressed and affected by the Meeting.

On the last great day of the Feast there was no preaching, but the day was spent in addressing the new converts, and in prayer. Before the Meeting was dismissed, all who loved the Lord Jesus Christ, and entertained the hope of glory, were requested to rise. About four-fifths of

the congregation rose ; the rest kept their seats.
It was a scene that bore away the mind irresisti-
bly to the Judgement of the Great Day. One
was taken and another left ; the husband was
separated from the wife, and the wife from the
husband ; parents rose up in the midst of their
children, while the children kept their seats in
silence.

The following hymn was then sung, and the
Meeting closed.

> " BLEST be the tie that binds
> Our hearts in Christian love :
> The fellowship of kindred minds,
> Is like to that above.
>
> Before our Father's throne
> We pour our ardent pray'rs :
> Our fears, our hopes, our aims are one,
> Our comforts and our cares.
>
> We share our mutual woes :
> Our mutual burthens bear :
> And often for each other flows,
> The sympathizing tear.
>
> When we asunder part,
> It gives us inward pain :
> But we shall still be joined in heart,
> And hope to meet again."

But it will be said, when such religious excitement subsides, what is left ?

I have conversed with some of the most
judicious and pious Americans on this subject—
with men who have had much to do with the
Revivals that have taken place in the United
States, during the last twenty or thirty years,

and it is their opinion, that although much of the excitement which is produced at Protracted Meetings soon dies away, still, those persons who are admitted to their several churches, after a proper interval of time, and with due examination, generally turn out consistent Christians; and often manifest a peculiar energy in religion, as if they received an impulse at Protracted Meetings which is not to be obtained under ordinary circumstances.

Several of those Christians, who were most active at the Meeting I have described, joined the church in consequence of a similar meeting at Vermillion, three or four years before; and they laboured and prayed for the conversion of sinners like men who attributed their own salvation, instrumentally, to the labours and prayers of other Christians at the former Meeting.

I resided two years at different places among Christians, many of whom were converted at such Meetings—I had daily opportunities of observing their spirit and conduct; and my own humble opinion on the subject is, that the ultimate effects of Protracted Meetings fully justify the means and measures used.

But it will be said again, How is it that Revivals in America are so transitory?

A similar enquiry produced the following reply of Dr. Beecher in his letter to the Editor of the New York Evangelist.

" Let them tell us

1. Not only how to disprove, but how to *eradicate* the opinion, that Revivals are and must be transient.

2. How to keep up a deep and humbling sense of our impotency to convert men, and dependence on the Holy Spirit, and the pressure of necessity, in the midst of abounding prosperity.

3. How to prevent the decline of gratitude, with the augmentation of spiritual mercies.

4. How to keep out self-complacency and spiritual pride, resulting from successful effort.

5. How to prevent the degeneracy of true into censorious zeal, in exhorting and reproving delinquent brethren.

6. How to find and keep the middle channel of habitual feeling and action up to, and not below, nor above, the exigencies of the work, and the enduring capacities of our nature.

7. How to shield the public mind from diversion, and the collisions of rival denominations.

8. How to prevent the intrusion of undefined, involuntary fear and apprehension, and make Christians, when they feel it, seal the lip, and go on praying, hoping, and acting as if they did not feel any fear.

9. How to make good men willing to work all the while, as devotedly in a revival, as they

must do to move the work on by God's blessing, up stream."

There is one more question, connected with the subject, which may be proposed. Notwithstanding the difference of circumstances, might not, and ought not means to be used for reviving religion in England, somewhat similar to those adopted by our brethren in America?

I humbly submit the question to the serious consideration of all who love our Lord Jesus Christ. And in conclusion, as we desire to see the glory of God promoted throughout the world, we shall rejoice to believe that pure and undefiled religion prevails in the woods and wilds of America. But a few years ago, the greater part of that country was an uninhabited wilderness. The seasons rolled round, but there was none to admire the varied wonders of creation, or riches of providence. The sun arose upon it and the rain descended; the trees blossomed, and scattered their fruits abroad; the rivers and lakes poured along their floods, and the cataracts thundered to the skies; but not a ray of intelligent glory was reflected to the Great Creator, not an eye that looked through nature up to nature's God, not a voice to hymn his praises. But now their wilderness is peopling with rational beings, and the God of salvation is meeting their spiritual wants, in the manner best adapted to their circumstances. Not only do Americans enjoy the outpourings of his Spirit, amidst the shades of their native forests, but many an Emigrant from England has met with mercy there; nor is the poor Indian forgotten.

" THE INDIAN HYMN.

In de dark woods, no Indian nigh,
Den me look Heb'n, and send up cry,
　　Upon my knee so low ;
But God on high, in shiny place,
See me at night wid teary face,—
　　De priest he tell me so.

God send he angel, take um care,
He come he self and hear um pray'r,
　　(If Indian heart do pray,)
He see me now, he know me here ;
He say poor Indian neber fear,
　　Me wid you night and day.

So me lub God, wid inside heart,
He fight for me, he take um part,
　　He save um life before :
God hear poor Indian in de wood,
So me lub him, and dat be good ;
　　Me pray him two times more.∗

∗ Meaning twice as often as formerly."

KETTERING :
PRINTED BY JOSEPH TOLLER.

R

LIST OF SUBSCRIBERS.

A.

Andrew, Mr. J. *Long Buckby* ..   ..   1 *copy.*

Andrews, Mrs. *Harlestone*   1

Ashby, Mrs. G. *Long Buckby*   1

Atchison, Mr. *Creaton*   1

B.

Barber, Rev. S. *Bridgenorth*   1

Barker, Mr. T. *East Haddon*   ..   1

Bates, Mr. T. *Long Buckby*   1

Beaumont, Mr. *Bridgenorth*   ..   1

Bayzand, Miss. *Ekington*   1

Benson, Mr. *Brington*   1

Birch, Mr. *London*   1

Brown, Mr. *Braunston*   1

Bland, Mr. J. *Reading*   1

Bland, Mr. W. *London*   1

Bunting, Mr. *Spratton* ..   ..   ..   1 *copy*.

Brewer, Mr. T. *London*   1

Bland, Mr. *Wellingborough*   1

Bland, Mr. J. *London*   1

Bourne, Mr. *Bridgenorth*   1

C.

Chamberlain, Mr. T. *East Haddon*..   1

Chapman, Mr. E. *ditto*   1

Chater, Rev. E. *Kibworth*   1

Capern, Rev. H. *Long Buckby*   ..   1

Clarke, Mr. J. *ditto*   1

Clarke, Mrs. *Rothwell*   1

Colley Mr. *Bridgenorth*   1

Corrie, Adam Esq. *Wellingborough*   ..   2 *copies*.

Coleman, Rev. T. *Ashley*   2

Cooper, Miss *Weedon*   3

Coleman, Mrs. *Chapel Brampton*   ..   1 *copy*.

Clarke, Mr. *London*   1

Chambers, Rev. J. *Willoughby*   ..   1

D.

Dix, Mr. *Long Buckby*..   ..   ..   1 *copy*.

Dickens, Miss M. *Ravensthorpe*   ..   1

Dickens, Miss A. *ditto*   1

Dawson, Mr. *London* ..   ..   ..   1 *copy.*

Dodd, Mr. *ditto*   1

Dunkley, Mr. *Rothersthorpe*   1

Devereux, Mr. J. *Long Buckby*   ..   1

Devereux, Mr. S. Warren *London* ..   1

E.

Eyre, Mr. *Long Buckby*   1

Edkins, Mr. *Bridgenorth*   1

Emerton, Mr. H. *Ravensthorpe*   ..   1

F.

Fifield, Mrs. *Rothwell*   1

Flavell, Miss, *Harleston*   1

G.

Gallard, Mr. R. *Long Buckby*   ..   1

Gamble, Mrs. *East Haddon*   1

Goodman, Miss A. *Long Buckby* ..   2 *copies.*

Goodman, Mr. *London* ..   ..   ..   1 *copy.*

Gardener, Mr. J. *Birmingham*   ..   1

Gaudern, Mr. *Creaton*   1

Goodrich, Rev. W. *Ravensthorpe* ..   3 *copies.*

Griffiths, Mr. W. *London*   2

Griffiths, Mrs. J. *ditto* ..   ..   ..   1 *copy.*

Griffiths, Miss A. *Bridgenorth*   ..   **1** *copy.*

Griffiths, Mr. G. *Long Buckby*   ..   1

H.

Hall, Mr. J. B. *Ravensthorpe*   ..   1

Hall, Mr. H. *ditto*   1

Halifax, Mrs. *East Haddon*   1

Heygate, Mr. J. *West Haddon*   ..   1

Harfard, Miss *Rothwell*   1

Hobbs, Miss *Birmingham*   .   ..   1

Hobson, Rev. B. *Welford*   1

Hudson, Mr. *Daventry*   1

Hubbard, Rev. C. B. *Banbury*   ..   1

I.

Islip, Rev. Mr. *Yelvertoft*   1

Islip, Mrs. *Rothwell*   1

Ivens, Mr. *Long Buckby*   1

J.

Johnson, Rev. S. *Wickhambrook*   ..   1

Johnson, Rev. J. *Farnham*   1

Johnson, Mr. S. *Northampton*   ..   1

Jones, Mr. *Bridgenorth*   1

L.

Lantsberry, Mr. W. *Spratton*   ..   1

Lantsberry, Mr. E. *Ravensthorpe* .. 1 *copy.*

Lantsberry, Mr. J. *ditto* 1

Lee, Mrs. *Leamington* 1

Linnell, Mr. W. *Ravensthorpe* .. 1

Loake, Mr. *Rothwell* 1

M.

Mabbott, Mr. *Long Buckby* 1

Mawby, Miss *ditto* 1

Marriott, Mr. *Norton* 1

Marriott, Miss *Long Buckby* 1

Mc. Michael, Mrs. Wyld *Bridgenorth* 1

Mercer, Mr. T. *Long Buckby* 1

Miller, Rev. Mr. *Braunston* 1

N.

Norton, Mr. *Bridgenorth* 1

P.

Paxon, W. Esq. *London* .. .. 2 *copies.*

Perkins, Mr. J, *Hillmorton* .. .. 1 *copy.*

Perkins, Miss. S. *Long Buckby* .. 1

Powell, Mr. T. *Ravensthorpe* .. 1

Potts, Mr. T. *Daventry* 1

Prust, Rev. Mr. *Northampton* .. .. 2 *copies.*

R.

Radburn, Mr. *Thorpe* ..   ..   ..   1 *copy.*

Robinson, Mr. *Buckby Lodge*   ..   1

Robinson, Mr. *East Haddon*   1

Robinson, Rev. W. *Kettering*   ..   1

Russell, Mr. *Buckby Lodge*   1

Russell, Mr, *Dodford*   1

Russell, Mr. J. *Priors Marston*   ..   1

Russell, Mr. W. *Dodford Mills* ..   1

Robinson, Mr. J. *Dunstable*   1

Rogers, Mrs. *Long Buckby*   ..   1

Robinson, Mr. W. *ditto*   1

Robins, Miss, *Birmingham*   ..   ..   2 *copies.*

S.

Sing, Mr. *Bridgenorth*   ..   ..   1 *copy.*

Southwell, Mr. *ditto*   1

South, Mr. R. *ditto*   1

Scott, Mrs. W. *Ravensthorpe*   1

Scott. Mr. T. *ditto*   1

Smith, Mr. W. *East Haddon*   ..   1

Smith, Mr. W. *ditto* ., ...   1

Smith, J. Buswell, *Lubenham*   1

Scott, Miss. *Rothwell*   1

Strange, Mr. *Yelvertoft* ..   ..   ..   1 *copy.*

Stuttend, Mr. *Banbury*   1

T.

Toller, Mrs. *Kettering*   1

Toller, Mr. R. *Leicester*   1

Toller, Mr. H. *Coward College, London*   1

U.

Underwood, Mr, *West Haddon*   ..   1

W.

Wadsworth, Mrs. J. *Long Buckby* ..   1

Warner, Mr. T. *Ravensthorpe*   1

White, Mr. R. *East Haddon*   ..   1

Williams, Sir James, *London* ..   ..   2 *copies.*

Williams, Rev. J. *Creaton*   2

Wykes, Mr. W. *ditto* ..   ..   ..   1 *copy.*

Wykes, Mr. J. *ditto*   1

Wyld Mrs. *Bridgenorth*   1

Williams, Rev. C. *Barby*   1